# Cute
# Little Store

*Between the entrepreneurial dream*

*and business reality*

## Adeena Mignogna

Outskirts Press, Inc.
Denver, Colorado

Outskirts Press
http://www.outskirtspress.com

ISBN-10: 1-59800-436-0
ISBN-13: 978-159800-436-6

# Table of Contents

# Preface:
# Why I wrote this book

I wrote this book to fill a gap. When I started my retail business in 2002, there were plenty of how-to-start-a-small-business books around. I probably own a copy of all of them by now.

There are also plenty of books out there by successful business folks. For example, *Pour Your Heart Into It* is about the success of Starbucks written by CEO Howard Schultz. Books like these can serve as a wonderful inspiration. (See the Appendix for a list of great books you should read if you're contemplating starting a small business.)

When my retail store first opened I was looking for something else. I was looking to read about businesses *like* mine. I wanted to read about people going through what I was going through. What happens in between the time when you get your business license and when you (hopefully) become wildly successful?

The knowledge in those first set of books on business start-ups seemed to stop when the business was up and running and the latter set of books skipped over the really hard parts of the day-to-day life and hardship of the new small business owner. Yes, Howard Schultz wrote about the early days of Starbucks, but he's writing with the knowledge that in the end, it worked. In the end, he wound up with a HUGE, successful corporation. Most people who write these types of books do so from the top of the mountain, not while they're making the climb.

Let's face reality: the majority of small businesses are lucky to be around after the first couple of years. The ones that survive the startup stage can be very successful and bring in a steady income to the owner. Knowledge about what that post-start-up-trying-to-keep-head-above-water-and-numbers-in-the-black stage… that's what I was looking for. So even though I found Mr. Schultz's story to be very inspiring (he came from nothing and "Look at me now, Ma!"), most of what he went through with Starbucks didn't feel like it applied to me and I didn't connect with it.

One of my passions has always been writing, so with not quite two years of retail under my belt, I decided to start writing about my business, The Pot & Bead, while all the problems and joys of new, small business ownership were, and still are, fresh. The wounds from my mistakes still stung, and the little joys of a great compliment or an awesome sales day still kept me going. As I finish this book, my store is approaching its fourth Anniversary.

I hope this book will serve as an inspiration to new small business owners who are also trying to survive their early years in business.

I also hope this book will fall into the hands of those thinking about going into business for themselves for the first time, particularly those going into a retail business. Retail is NOT easy. It requires LOTS of hard work and dedication and sacrifices in terms of income, family, and time. Many people think of retail as a "build it and they will come" type of business. That's simply not true. This book should serve as an insight into what really happens in that Cute Little Store.

I'd like to thank just about everybody in my life who has helped me in my career, at The Pot & Bead, and with this book. This especially includes my parents, my boyfriend, my ex-husband, and all the employees (past and present) at my store. I also want to thank the people who took time out of their lives to act as reviewers and editors for this book: Raymond Mignogna, Dave Kenyon, and Alix Inchausti.

# Introduction

"Entrepreneurship is working 80 hours a week so you don't have to work 40 for anyone else." - Corporate CEO Ramona Arnett

The purpose of this book is to give you some idea of what to expect if you decide to become a small business owner. It might, however, convince some people not to go into business for themselves.

Let's examine the statistics. In 2004, it was estimated that 580,900 new small businesses ("new firms" according to the U.S. Small Business Administration) were created. But in that same year, there were approximately 576,200 closures and 34,317 bankruptcies. In 2002 and 2003, there were also more closures than there were new firms.

The SBA maintains a website (www.sba.gov) that anyone contemplating starting a new business should use as a source of research. If you browse through the "Office of Advocacy" section (that's a good source for small business statistics) their FAQ page states that:

"Two-thirds of new employer establishments survive at least two years, and 44 percent survive at least four years, according to a new study. These results were similar for different industries...

Earlier research has explored the reasons for a new business's survivability. Major factors in a firm's remaining open include an ample supply of capital, the fact that a firm is large enough to have employees, the owner's education level, and the owner's reason for starting the firm in the first place, such as freedom for family life or wanting to be one's own boss."

It's those first couple of years that can make or break a business. At the time I started my business, many other people started theirs. I'm still in business while they're not.

I hope that by writing this, I can give you some insight into what really goes on "behind the scenes." I call it "behind the scenes" because ideally, your customer only sees your best – they should have no idea how much stress and aggravation you're really going through. The downside is that when customers see what I call the "Cute Little Store," it looks like something they can do too, and many times, they do.

I don't want you to be one of those who see the good side and decide to open a business based on just that - only to have it fail. If it fails, you can potentially lose a lot of money, affect the lives and well-being of your spouse and kids, as well as affecting the rest of your own future.

When I started writing this book, The Pot & Bead had been open about a year and a half and my business wasn't 100% out of that early, risky time period. My business had already survived a lot of unexpected occurrences and hardships, but I knew we would make it.

As I finish this book, we've been open more than three years and it looks like we will be in the 44% that the SBA says make it to 4 years!

Why are we surviving while others aren't? I believe it's a combination of a LOT of upfront preparation work and a good dose of luck. For example, some days I sit and think how lucky we are to have the location we have. But then I remember how we got there: all the places we looked at that weren't quite right, examining the demographic numbers of all the possible locations, getting information from other businesses similar to ours across the country, etc. So it was luck that the right place existed, but a lot of work to determine it was the right place, negotiate and sign the lease, and keep it going.

I've written some articles and talked to some folks about the perils of business ownership. I've occasionally been criticized for being depressing. I prefer to look at it as inserting a dose of reality. That's because it's not all good stuff – it's not all fun and games.

Around the time I started writing this book, I spoke with a customer who, while she was sitting in my shop, told me about how she was thinking of opening up a store of her own (not like mine). She and a friend had recently been laid off and were thinking that this might be their opportunity to go out on their own. I'm always willing to talk to people about my experiences in starting up a business, and I'm always willing to refer people to the resources I've used (accountant, lawyer, local Small Business Development Center, etc.).

Well, the perception she (and a lot of other people) have is that not only is my business doing well, but that I am personally financially successful. I explained to her that yes, the business is doing well, but that no, I am personally not receiving much financial benefit. That shocked her. She wasn't sure she'd be able to handle the drop in compensation and has since reconsidered her desire to open her own store.

I started writing this chapter in the middle of 2004. At that time, I expected to take home *maybe* a fifth of what my salary was when I was an engineer. It turned out to be less than that come the end of the year.

I took an informal survey of people I know who are in a similar type of retail business as mine: Only 15% were able to say that their salary was $30k a year or more, while 12% said they were not paying themselves anything. That leaves about 70% who are paying themselves less than $30k a year!

In the chapter on money, I go into a little more detail on some of the monetary issues the small business owner must deal with before s/he can think about paying him or herself.

Basically, I don't want you to wind up in the same situation as these folks:

One retail business owner I know closed his doors after only a year. He estimates that he is $100k in the hole. This money was spent mostly on furnishing the retail space and paying rent.

Another retail business owner I know decided that this wasn't for her and figured she would try and sell the business after being open for a year and a few months. After about 7-8 months on the market, she sold it for a steal. After everything was said and done, she wound up about $10k in debt. I think what upset her more is the toll this had taken on her two young girls. She told me once while she was in the process of selling her business: "I haven't been able to give either of them a birthday party in two years!"

Read this book and think about all the hard questions you'll need to ask yourself while you plan your business. (Why do you want to own your own business? Do you require a certain salary to support yourself and your family?)

This book should either inspire you or have you saying "Oh, wow, I had no idea it was like that." Each of the following chapters should provide some insight into the different aspects of owning and running a retail business.

# Chapter 1: The Pot & Bead: A New Life

What prompts a seemingly normal engineer to up and quit her day job and open a retail business?

This chapter gives the background story to my successful retail store, The Pot & Bead, a contemporary Paint-Your-Own-Pottery studio located in Ashburn, VA. I'll discuss how the lessons I've learned are applicable to almost any retail business and to new, small businesses in general.

# Chapter 2: You Want to Do *What!?* Perceptions of Retail

When you own and run a Cute Little Store you'll often overhear customers say how they wish they had something like it. As a store owner, there's an amazing mix of emotions resonating through your body all at once that could almost prompt a meltdown:

1. You're flattered. It's nice to hear that they like your store.
2. You're chuckling inside. If they only knew how much work it took to have the Cute Little Store.
3. Your blood is boiling a little. Are they going to try and open something just like it right down the street?

People have their perceptions, often misconceptions, about what retail is and what it takes to run a retail business. This chapter discusses those ideas.

# Chapter 3: Leasing, Landlords, and Opening Late

This chapter tells the tale of obtaining the lease for the location of The Pot & Bead and all the trials and tribulations involved. It's a lesson in research, following your instincts, and negotiating.

## Chapter 4: Safe and Secure

Burglaries can happen. It did happen to us. We survived. There were things that could have been done to prevent our burglary that I wish I had known then. I'll tell you all those things in this chapter so it hopefully won't happen to you too. Protecting your business, from burglaries and other disasters, is a must for business owners.

## Chapter 5: Employees

When I counsel people about starting a new business, I remind them that one enormous difference between a home-based business and a retail business is the need for employees. A retail business needs and depends on its employees.

As the owner of a *successful* retail business, you *can't* be there all the hours, every single day. (Okay, you can, but you probably will wind up resenting it.) So do you just hire someone and hope to hell that when you're not there everything will go just fine? Almost. In this chapter, we'll talk about how to hire, retain, and treat your employees.

## Chapter 6: Follow Your Gut

This chapter talks about the biggest mistake I made in the first two years of running The Pot & Bead. I attempted to purchase another business similar to my own. It didn't go well and I lost a lot of money. Why? I didn't follow my gut.

## Chapter 7: Customers… Ya Gotta Love Them

In this chapter, I will teach you to recite the mantra "I love my customers, I love my customers."

I define *customer* as "someone who gives me money." Without them, I wouldn't be in business. I love my customers.

This chapter is the support room for getting past the few

customers who are crazy or just plain mean, and will help show you how to appreciate the nice customers who make the business worthwhile.

Chapter 8: Competition

I define *competition* as "someone who takes *my* money from *my* customers."

Who is "the competition?" Why should you care? How do you deal with it? This chapter answers these questions.

Chapter 9: They Gotta Know You're There

The bulk of the on-going work in a retail (or any) business is marketing. Unleash your creative side and have at it, but wait a while to see the results.

Chapter 10: Hard Work Does Not Equal Money In Your Pocket

Admit it. This is one of the top reasons you want to be in business for yourself. You want to make more money than you have right now. Until that happens, you might have to borrow some, will definitely have to spend some, and will hopefully collect large piles of it at the end of the day.

Chapter 11: Other Things That Keep You Up At Night

This chapter discusses some of the other random things that go wrong in day-to-day business. This will largely involve all the stuff that breaks, the weather and my own arch-nemesis, Water.

Chapter 12: How To Survive Those First Two Years

In this chapter, I will give some useful information for get-

ting through the start-up phase of any business, but particularly retail. It will include basic information on:
- Business planning
- Organization
- Your Team of Experts
- Building a Support System
- Putting Your Personal Finances in Order
- Keeping Yourself Healthy
- Stress Relieving and Sanity Keeping Techniques

Chapter 13: So You Still Want Your Own Cute Little Store

You're still convinced that a retail business is your next professional career move. This chapter is a checklist, to help make sure you're ready and that you don't repeat others' past, deadly mistakes.

If you do decide to go ahead with your eyes wide open and the advice in this book, you may end up with your own successful Cute Little Store!

# Chapter 1
## The Pot & Bead: A New Life

Hi, my name is Adeena and I own a small business. You would think that there would be a psychiatric support group for small business owners. The amount of time, effort, and work borders on the masochistic. The sacrifices are great. But at the end of the day, the rewards can be even greater. Yet you have to wonder about people who start their own businesses... no matter who they are or where they come from, the odds are undoubtedly stacked against them.

That was certainly true in my case. I had a nice, neat little career as an engineer in aerospace, a field I had been interested in since I was a small child. I'm basically a complete science geek. That was the only side of me most people ever knew about. I worked on designing and operating satellites, dreamed about being an astronaut, and read science magazines and science books all the time. So a lot of folks I knew were baffled by my desire to not only work for myself, but to work in a completely different field.

However, those who really know me, my family and close, old friends, know entrepreneurship was always something on my mind and something I knew I would do one day. At the end of the day, I needed to be the one calling the shots. I've always known that the only way I would have great rewards in life and be happy would be by taking great risks.

I'm sure those last two sentences ring true for a lot of you reading this book. You're ready to take that risk (or you've already started), you know the odds are stacked against you, and you're looking for some moral support. You want to know how others have dealt with the first difficult years of owning their own business.

There are lots of books you can (and should) read about starting your own business. (See Appendix A: The Reading List) There are books that cover the how-to, the legalities, where to get money, and other things. Many books tell you *how* to start a business, not many deal with what happens right after you've made that leap. This book will tell you about all the little pitfalls that happen along the way and how to not let those pitfalls get in the way of your success.

This book, while focusing on retail businesses, can and does apply to any business in those first couple of years. No matter who you are or what type of business you have, you'll hit some snags along the way. I'm here to tell you to read on and hang in there! You'll make it through! You have a dream, you have a goal and you can do it!

I always knew I wanted to work for myself. I also always knew I wanted to work in the space industry or *in space*. When I was about 6 years old, I knew that when I grew up, I would own my own company. We would build robots. And we'd be doing this on the moon. (At the time, I didn't know that we hadn't been to the moon in a while, I thought we went there every day.)

While in elementary school, I would dream about being called "president." I knew about college and believed that I needed to get advanced degrees in a science (computer science and robotics were at the top of my list back then) and in business. I would make pretend business cards for myself. I even started a couple little businesses... I had a lemonade stand set up at the end of the driveway, and at one point collected rocks off the beach, polished them, gave them cute names, and attempted to sell them as display pieces.

As I grew older, my goals became a little more in tune with reality. I still wanted a career in the space industry. And I still wanted to own my own company.

I went to school at the University of Maryland and earned degrees in Physics and Astronomy. (Cute Little Tidbit: A lot of folks have asked why not just major in Aerospace Engineering. Well, when I was nearing the end of high school, folks who were graduating with Aerospace Engineering degrees were still having a tough time finding jobs in their field. I thought that if I got my degree in AE, I would be trapped into something very narrow. I note this because at times in this book I talk about understanding your own strengths and weaknesses and one of mine is that I'm not very detail minded for very long. Narrowing myself into one little niche for 20 years, while exciting to some, brings on something akin to a claustrophobia attack when I think about it.)

My physics professor in high school had his undergraduate and graduate degrees in Physics. During the course of his lifetime he had done a little of everything: he worked as an engineer, he worked as an astronomer, he worked for different companies doing different things, he taught and now I believe he's writing too. So I wound up seeing physics as something that could lead me to a lot of options afterwards. Keeping my options open, not cutting off any opportunities, is something I've always seen as the right thing to do.

3

During college I worked in a group at the University doing mechanical design and drafting. I was very lucky. At the time, the work I was doing was exactly what I believed I wanted to do during my career after college. We were designing and building a scientific instrument that would go on to sit on a satellite and study the Sun.

Is this relevant to owning your own business? Yes, most definitely! It relates to knowing yourself. I like to create. I like to do new things and make new things. I like to start with nothing, and wind up with something to show for the work I've done.

Entrepreneurship also takes quite a bit of creativity and the desire to make something where there was nothing before.

This is only one facet of entrepreneurship. There are other attributes that go into making an entrepreneur. I'm convinced that in order to be successful, you don't need to possess *all* the traits yourself, but you do need to be able to know which ones you have and which ones you don't. For the ones you don't, you need to be able to find others who do have those skills to supplement you. (See Chapter 12: How To Survive Those First Two Years)

After college I worked for several years in various space-related engineering jobs. While working the day job, I tried to be a consultant on the side. I was a computer aided design (CAD) drafter. I had the proper software and computer equipment I needed at home. I had the know-how and I even had some apropos business cards printed up (They looked like a blueprint – quite charming if I do say so myself.)

The CAD consulting thing didn't work out too well. The 40+ hour a week day job interfered with my ability to find consulting work – consultant-entrepreneurs need to devote a significant portion of their time to selling themselves and marketing their own services. I didn't have the time or money to invest in this part of a business back then, so I wound up doing only one job as a CAD consultant. (A couple years later, I was lucky enough to be in the right place at the right time and did a couple software consulting jobs, but it was pure luck that got me the gig – it wasn't enough to really make it as an independent consultant.)

In the day-job career, I progressed to smaller and smaller companies moving a little closer to management in each company. I learned more and more about financial matters, business, sales, marketing, etc. I knew I wanted my own aerospace company and I *knew* it was just a matter of being prepared when the right idea and right opportunity hit me. I read books, I talked to people, I even thought about going back to school part time to earn an MBA.

All that time I was keeping my eyes open for that idea that would lead me to break away and start my own company. I amassed a decent collection of "How to Start Your Own Business" books.

Well, I was certainly learning a lot. The biggest thing was that commercial aerospace was not making a ton of money. Who wants to buy a small satellite? Anyone? Anyone? It was very hard to keep a small company going.

What really opened my eyes was this: The last company I worked for, in its hey-day, had about 60 employees and 2 main contracts (i.e., customers). Instead of doing some good engineering work, a lot of my job was fighting to keep one of those customers happy so they would continue to pay us. Why? Because if they went away, we would have to cut everyone's pay, or lay people off, or even close our doors!

This didn't make a lot of good business sense to me. Yes, it is very important to keep your customers happy… absolutely! But what if just focusing on customers' happiness in the moment means you're not focusing on getting the real job done? Giving them the lollypop they asked for now might ruin the special dinner you promised them at the end of the day. (I was starting to have a lot of issues and arguments with my managers… no, I didn't have as much experience as they did, but the way they acted and made decisions just didn't seem to make common sense.)

A lot of independent consultants I know are in a similar boat. They're dedicated to one or two customers at a time – and need to keep those customers to keep themselves in business. That leaves little time to find the next customer. Most consultants in this situation will have on/off work and inconsistent money coming in. That wasn't a life that sat well with me. It was at this point that I truly gave up the idea that I would be a consultant in my spare time or give up the day job to start a consulting business.

For those of you who are comfortable with, and able to live that kind of life, more power to you! There are some definite advantages to that kind of entrepreneurship. The potential to work out of your house is one of them. Later in this book I talk about some of the horrors I've endured in renting retail space. After dealing with that, I'd probably give my right leg (maybe not a leg, but at least a pinky toe) to be able to solely work from my home office.

When I finally realized that having a small aerospace company was not likely in the near future I looked for something else. After I had bought every how-to-start-a-small-business book I could find, I then started collecting and reading all those how-to-start-a-_____ (fill-in-the-blank) kind of business – everything from coffee bar to restaurant to real estate.

It happened one day that I came across the Paint-Your-Own-Pottery (PYOP) concept. One of my sisters had recently painted me a small dish as a wedding present. It was in the shape of a half moon (she knows how I'm into everything "spacey") and she had painted a light blue background with a face onto it. It was my favorite wedding gift and it still hangs on the wall in my living room.

I was sitting, having coffee, in Starbucks one day with my soon-to-be business partner, and he was ranting excessively about how people don't give handmade gifts anymore. I corrected him by telling him about that dish my sister painted for me. I also mentioned that she'd taken my young niece a bunch of times to paint for our parents. (There's a very colorful figurine in the shape of a snake sitting in my dad's office, a fish on their mantle, and at least one picture frame in the dining room.)

My partner then recalled that he had taken his daughters to some places like that back when they lived on the west coast. That was the light bulb. It was so bright I think it filled the room.

How did I know this was the right idea for me? Well, at this point, I was already very familiar with business plan writing and already knew a little about finding financing. Remember all those books I'd collected? Well each time I started looking into an idea, like the coffee bar or real estate business, I would start writing the business plan. When the plan didn't seem to go anywhere, I'd stop and move on to the next idea.

I was just waiting for the right idea to come along and fit in. The more I started researching the Paint-Your-Own-Pottery (PYOP) concept, the more my gut told me that this was the right thing to do.

About seven months after starting the business plan for The Pot & Bead, we were open for business.

When discussing the early part of this business, I'll sometimes use the word "I" and sometimes use the word "we." That's because I did initially start the business with a partner. When I started writing this book, I was also in the early process of buying him out. It took the better part of a year for that process to complete and as I finish this book, it's been over for more than a year. I was extremely lucky – I've heard many buy-out horror stories and even though it took a lot of time, it was relatively painless. To protect his identity, I will call him John for the remainder of the book.

John and I worked together as engineers. We were both fed up with the lifestyle of working for others and had similar ideas about what we wanted to do. They say that you shouldn't go into business with your friends. Well, we were colleagues working together before we were friends, so it seemed okay.

Did I need a partner to start this business? Yes and no. Looking back now, I absolutely, 100% believe that I could have done all this on my own. But I think he was the extra push that got me out the door. (There is also the question about whether I needed him for the business loan process or not. Securing the business loan might have been a little more difficult without the additional person and additional collateral.)

Most entrepreneurs, when they tell friends and family of the risks they're about to take, are met with a lot of negativity:

- "You want to do what!?"
- "Where are you going to get the money for that!?"
- "But you don't know anything about that."
- "You're making good money now, why would you want to change that?"

I certainly had my share coming from friends and family. I think my ex-husband said each one of those statements to me. (After a year of being in business, however, he apologized for the negative comments and tried to explain that he only knew me as "space-geek," so this was a complete shock to him.)

John was that one extra person saying "Yes, we can do it!" and I think I needed that at the time.

The partnership did eventually die. Our initial plan was that I would manage the business and he would help out when and where he could. This was done out of necessity. I was able to quit my day job. With a family of young kids to support, John wasn't. Shortly after the business opened, his job and family situation changed to the point that he could not be a part of the business as we envisioned. It became an unfair situation and necessitated me buying him out.

Here's the thing we did right: when we set up our business entity, we had a lawyer prepare a pretty iron-clad operating agreement between John and myself. This helped make the buy-out much more straightforward and amicable. An operating agreement is a document that outlines what each partner is coming to the table with, and discusses what happens if a partner wants to leave, or worse, dies.

Many, many businesses that start out as partnerships often end up this way. We had the best intentions going in, and it just didn't work. If you have a partner, no matter what stage your business is in, make sure you also have an operating agreement drawn up by an attorney or other neutral party.

After many lessons learned, these days I would never recommend doing anything this important without the aid of a good lawyer. (See Chapter 6 on my mistakes in not using a lawyer.) But if you really, truly feel you can't afford one to do an operating agreement, make sure you have at least *something* written down. Handbooks on legal forms for small business can act as a guide, and can be useful if you really can't afford a lawyer. (See the Reading List in Appendix A.)

So what is The Pot & Bead? We are a paint-your-own-pottery and bead-your-own-jewelry craft studio. Customers can come in any time we're open, pick out a "blank" piece of pottery, also known as "bisque," paint it, and leave it with us to glaze and fire in a kiln. Customers get the pottery back one week later and it's food, microwave, and dishwasher safe.

Customers can also come in to bead jewelry. They can make necklaces, bracelets, anklets, and more. We do all the "hard" stuff, such as attaching the clasps. The customers pick out beads and string 'em. The best thing is, they get to wear their creations home that day.

We also host parties. Mostly for kid's birthdays, but we host adult parties, teambuilding parties, scout troops, and more. Party guests paint or bead, have some cake and have a great time!

(Cute Little Tidbit: Look at the above three paragraphs that describe The Pot & Bead. I can say those sentences (without talking too fast) in a little less than 60 seconds. EVERY business owner should have a similar 60-second elevator speech memorized that describes their business. I can't tell you how many business owners I've met that really are not able to articulate what they do – at least not before I'm bored and ready to talk with someone else.)

(Another Cute Little Tidbit: The paint-your-own-pottery concept isn't original. But opening a pottery studio that is *also* a beading studio is original. At least it was at the time. Yes, there were one or two others that offered beading, but ours was the first studio to open with both activities as core to our business. The point here is, even if you find an idea that's been done, you can tweak it and make it your own.)

The Good:
- You can learn from and apply any previous experience.
- There's a great feeling of satisfaction that comes from owning your own business – from knowing you can do it.

The Bad:
- Going into business for yourself is a risk!
- If you try something that doesn't fit who you are, you might waste a lot of time and money.

A Final Tidbit:
Know thyself and the business you're getting involved in.

# Chapter 2

## You Want to Do *What!?* Perceptions of Retail

One of the first people I told about The Pot & Bead idea was my dad. He wasn't shocked about the idea of going out on my own. He's tried the entrepreneurial route more than once and I've had several conversations with him over the years about my frustrations with my career and working for myself. He was however, surprised that it was a retail business I was interested in.

My family hasn't had super success with entrepreneurship, and retail in particular was looked down upon ever since an uncle of mine went bankrupt in the mid-80's after opening up a card shop. Retail was thought to be too risky. You can be ruined by picking the wrong location, as my uncle did.

My dad wound up giving me one piece of very good advice: learn from the mistakes of others. This is a key message I hope that you'll pick up on too.

There is one main distinction I want to make here. Yes, I own a "pottery studio," but the business I'm really in is retail. There is a difference. There are artists and other good people that own a pottery studio. These are often characterized by:

- being located in an out of the way place
- an owner who doesn't take or doesn't need to take a salary OR breaks even but isn't making tons of money
- not having many employees
- owners who spend the majority of their time on their art, not on building the business

There is *nothing* wrong with this if this is the lifestyle you choose. This is not the business I'm in or what I do. I'm in retail. I characterize this by:

- being located in a highly visible shopping plaza, in the middle of our key customer demographic
- having a store manager (most of the time; more about troubles on keeping a good manager in Chapter 5) and several part-time employees
- my time being spent on marketing and building the business. Increasing sales from quarter to quarter and year to year is a priority.

This is a *business* – not a hobby or a vocation.

The purpose of pointing this out is to let you know that neither I nor my employees sit around painting pottery all day. Many a customer in my store has said something to the effect of: "It must be great to work here! You get to sit around and paint pottery all day!" at which point we politely correct them. The work we do enables *customers* to sit around and paint pottery all day. Just like Starbucks employees don't sit around drinking coffee all day... they're doing other things so that their customers reap those benefits.

Now, I do want my customers to think of my store as that Cute Little Store that they come to. They should think all is well. When customers are at my store, they should be able to relax and forget about their problems and not be burdened with mine.

The downside is that customers have a false perception of my business. For the most part, that's okay. Most customers don't need to know anything about the business. What happens behind the scenes is not relevant to their ability to enjoy the service and products we provide.

Occasionally, the Cute Little Store gives a customer false hope. Everything goes so well for them; we make it seem easy and they wind up thinking they can do it too, or even better. That in itself is not so bad. All of us probably sees something and dreams of having it or doing it. (I'm a big fan of cute little coffee shops, tea rooms, and bookstores and dream of owning them when I visit.) The problem occurs when the customer, based only on their experience in the store, skips a large amount of research, or performs the research with those awful rose-colored glasses and thinks it'll be so easy to do. This is exactly the trap I'm trying to warn you about.

Have you been in one of these stores? Maybe it was a Cute Little Store in a vacation spot. Maybe it was an independent bookstore - you've thought about having one yourself. If you're a book lover, maybe you've thought about being surrounded by your favorite titles all day, able to share your knowledge with other people about the best authors and your favorite classics.

The reality is that in order to keep that store open, (and hopefully pay yourself) what you really need to be concerned with is how many books you have to sell every month to make your lease payment. Having gobs of knowledge about the books (aka, your product) is of great value to customer service, but at the end of the day, you have to make the sale to stay in business. I have to sell approximately 250-300 pieces of pottery just to pay the rent each month. And rent is only about 20% of my monthly expenses (more in Chapter 10 about Money).

Somewhere not too far away in Pennsylvania, there was this wonderful little coffee shop. It was set in an old historic house on the edge of a touristy little town complete with adorable bed & breakfasts, antique shops, and the like. You'd think a coffee shop would fit in just perfectly. Each room was very cozy and you could take your time sipping your latte on one of several comfy couches. You could borrow a book to read while having your tea on the side porch. It was relaxing, it was cozy, and they made delicious coffee. It was the kind of shop lots of people like you and me would love to own.

But after a couple visits to this shop, I had some conversations with the managers and was able to find out that they were having huge problems selling enough coffee to keep the doors open. In addition, it turns out they weren't very welcome in the town either. They believed that the local town Chamber of Commerce was made up of a lot of people who had something against this new coffee shop (even though it wasn't competing with an existing one) which made it difficult to market in the town.

Why did the local people not like the coffee shop? I really don't know – and the information I received from the managers might have been colored by their own exhaustion and despair. This is just one example of an unexpected hardship a business could face.

I'm not sure if they're still in business – it wasn't looking good the last time I passed by.

Lots of customers walk into my store during a busy time and say something like the following: "Wow, you're so busy! Things must be going well, eh?" And on more than one occasion, a bolder customer will even say something like "You must be doing very well," and I take their meaning to be that I personally am doing well financially.

To the first customer, I'll always be nice and polite and chipper and say, "Yes, things are good," and smile.

To the latter, I'm more careful with how I respond. A lot

of the time it will have to do with my mood, if the customer is a regular whom I know, or if I think they have that look in their eye thinking they can make a lot of money with a Cute Little Store too.

Usually, my response is something simple like "Well, sales are good." On occasion I've gotten into small discussions about how even though sales are good, that doesn't mean I'm raking it in hand-over-fist. I'll sometimes say, "Yes, sales are good, but they need to be because this is an expensive area to keep a business." Usually that's enough for the person to understand.

The county that my business is in is home to LOTS of small businesses and entrepreneurs. Many times I will have a more frank discussion with someone looking to go into business for themselves. I'm a very positive person so I don't want to talk them out of it, or be one of those negative people telling them they shouldn't do it. I also don't want to give away too much information about my own business. But I will always tell them about some of the resources I used when getting started, like the local Small Business Development Center (SBDC). (See Chapter 12: How To Survive Those First Two Years)

I'll also tell them that I'm not making much money at all, that I have no kids (allowing me more time to do what I want to do) and that I work A LOT.

Before ending this chapter, I want to talk about one other misconception of retail: free time. I've noticed that a lot of people who have yet to own their own business think that doing so gives them more free time, including more time to spend with their kids and family. While this might be true for home-based businesses, it is NOT true for cute little retail shops.

A lot of retail shops are open seven days a week. During the first few months we were open I was at my shop every day. It was somewhere in the second month when I felt I had the staff trained enough so that I could go home early one evening.

I was someone who committed myself to getting staff in place so I could do just that. Other retail owners aren't so fortunate, or simply don't plan for that.

Even after having the staff trained properly so they can run the place, you can never be completely not there. Your presence is still needed and you need to decide when you should be there: the busiest times, of course. For my store, like a lot of others, the busiest times are the weekends. If I had kids, that would mean I'd be missing soccer games, play time, and, in general, the times when my kids would be home.

So if you're thinking you want a Cute Little Store so you have more time for your family, please look at other alternatives.

If you've been in a store recently and said to yourself that you want to own a Cute Little Store too, ponder over these questions:

- Do I like what the store sells or would I like providing it to others?
- Can I work seven days a week? (and do the same thing day after day after day?)
- How much do I have to sell to make rent and other expenses?
- What is it about this store that I really like?

The Good:
- Pride in ownership; being your own boss; calling the shots.
- With a lot of time and hard work (and possibly money), owning your own business can be a reality.

The Bad:
- Small (possibly tiny, miniscule) income.
- Time not spent with friends and family.

Final Tidbits:

Know what kind of person you are. Are you detail oriented or do you only want to focus on the big picture? Do you thrive on routine, or does doing the same thing day after day after day make you want to pull you hair out? Think about who you are and think about how this fits in with the business you're in (or want to be in).

# Chapter 3
Leasing, Landlords, and Opening Late

"Location, location, location." That's the mantra we've all heard. And yes, it's true. Location is VERY important to a retail business.

When my partner and I were first planning The Pot & Bead, our idea was that it would be in a quaint, historic-y area. After all, lots of pottery studios were in quaint, historic districts, and the rent would be cheaper there than in a strip mall or shopping plaza. (If you're familiar with Loudoun County, Virginia, we were looking in the historic district of Leesburg.)

First, I should point out that we didn't know a thing about leasing space for a business. Books helped a little... they explained some of the terminology like CAM or Triple Net and other things to expect in a commercial lease. (See Appendix A)

We spent a couple of months looking at different spaces available in the historic district. The rents were all reasonable, but none of the spaces were right. They were either too small, or not on the ground floor, or didn't have a bathroom. None of them had good parking. It was frustrating and there were times we were tempted to settle for something that wasn't quite right.

A new part of an upscale shopping center was in the process of being built at that time in the next town over. At first, while sitting at this center's Starbucks, we thought it was going to be prohibitively expensive. But on the other hand, we would be getting the right amount of space, good parking, road visibility, a bathroom... what more could we want? It all seemed to be coming together perfectly.

One of the first major decisions we faced was deciding between a space on the "bottom floor," which faced into the main part of the shopping center, and a space on the "top floor," which faced outside the shopping center, but onto main roads. The rent on the "top floor" would be slightly less expensive than the bottom. When I say "top floor," though, we're not on the top where you need to take stairs or an elevator to get to us. The "top floor" has its own parking lot.

My partner John and I argued quite a bit about this. He wanted to be downstairs facing into the shopping center and I wanted to be upstairs with the cheaper rent and facing the roads. In the end, I won (because of the cheaper rent), and it turned out to be the right decision. Even though the "bottom" floor faces into the main part of the shopping center, it's far enough away from the "anchor" (usually a big store like a grocery store) that it doesn't help much.

Up on "the top," almost half of our customers said they found out about us in the first year and a half we were open by driving by on the road we face.

Given that most of our customers have young kids and drive an SUV or mini-van, having the parking out front is very important.

The lease negotiations went well. Too well. Looking

back, we didn't negotiate hard enough. We were so excited about getting the location that we didn't ask for enough and we took a lot of the things that the landlord said for granted.

For one, we were supposed to be the last business open on our floor of the shopping center. We turned out to be the first one open. Why is this important? We had to do extra work to let everyone know we were there.

There were a lot of questions we didn't ask during the lease review process but should have. Some were:

- "What if the toilet breaks in the first couple months? Who's responsible for that?"
- "Do we get a tenant allowance for build-outs?"
- "What is the landscaping plan?" (Trees were planted at one of the parking lot ends that, when fully grown, will make it difficult for people driving by to see us from the road.)

We might not have gotten the answer we wanted to each of these questions, but it's still always better to have asked.

After taking possession of the space, the relationship between me and the landlord was pretty adversarial for a long while. Currently, my #1 risk (and fear) for the future of my business is what will happen when it's time to re-negotiate the lease. It's a risk point right now because the landlord doesn't have to renew our lease or make the conditions favorable for us. Yes, the lease has a "five-year option," but that doesn't automatically mean my business will be able to exist in the same space, at close to the same rent, for another five years. Read up on commercial leases so you understand what this means. (See Appendix A.)

What do they say about hindsight? Knowing what I know now, I wish we had asked for or signed a ten-year lease instead of five (Note that I'm not recommending this.) But that would have been a different kind of risk taken at a time when we didn't know if the business was going to succeed at all – breaking a commercial lease is not something you want to have to do. The terms are almost never favorable to the tenant.

We've had a variety of problems with the physical space and lease since the store opened. They ranged from "mild headache" to "oh-my-god this is going to shut us down":

- The windows: We're not allowed to put a sign in our back window that says we're here. So, many customers in the shopping center have problems finding us. Not a day goes by where we don't get at least one or two calls from customers saying they're lost in the shopping center.

- Common Area Maintenance (CAM) increases: In addition to your rent, you typically also pay something called CAM or triple-net. This covers the maintenance costs like landscaping and snow removal in your shopping center. It's typically not fixed – it goes up and down each year based on the real cost from the year before. Also, when they figure out whether or not it goes up or down, they can charge you a one time pay-ment to cover the previous year's actual costs (or give you a credit if costs were less than expected). Well, after the first full year, when our assessment came in, we owed an assessment of almost twice our rent! It was a lot of money at the time and completely outrageous. It almost put us out of business.

- Snow Removal: Our first winter brought a huge snow storm, and even though we were required to be open, the snow removal in our parking lot was miserable. We got phone calls from several customers saying they tried to get to us but couldn't. In just two or three days, I estimate we lost at least $500 of business just from the people who *told* us they couldn't get through. I don't want to think about how many couldn't get through that we don't know about.

- Lights: We had to call several times to get the landlord

to turn the lights in the parking lot on after dark. (This situation repeats every time daylight savings ends.)

- Proof of Insurance: For almost three years, I kept getting letters saying that the landlord needed proof of my insurance. I'd faxed that proof over several times and still received these letters. (This finally stopped after we had been open almost three years.)
- Muzak: We had a Musak system installed our first year. This required putting an antenna on the roof. It took two months for the property manager to get back to Muzak with the approval and instructions for doing this.

Am I just complaining here? No. (Although it does feel good to vent a little – aaaaahhhhhh.) I'm trying to make you aware of all those little and big things that happen while running your business. These are things that you don't necessarily have any control over and can: 1) give you a headache, 2) cause you to lose business, 3) give you an ulcer, 4) potentially close you down, or 5) all of the above.

Someone recently asked me if I did this all over again, would I want to own my space. The answer is maybe. (It's not easy to give a definitive "yes" or "no" since there are always other factors to consider.)

If I was turning back the clock on The Pot & Bead, owning my own space, while giving me a lot more control would have presented an entirely different risk. We likely would not have been able to be in such a visible area with good parking. We certainly wouldn't have been able to open when we did since construction at our location was already near completion when we signed the lease.

But, knowing what I know now, if I ever looked into being in another, different retail business, I would likely want to own my own land and space. Although, if I did this, I would probably just want to be the landlord and not actually run a retail business.

For anyone considering retail, owning the space is something definitely worth researching. It's a tangible asset that you still own even if the business doesn't succeed.

Once you have your lease (or mortgage, if you've decided to buy your space), it's time to prepare for your Cute Little Store.

Christmas, like it is for a lot of retailers, is supposed to be our busiest time of year. So, we were very interested in making sure we were open in time for the season. Originally, we planned on taking possession of the space sometime in early to mid-September, (when the building would be finished) and opening at the very beginning of October. (I should point out that during negotiations, the landlord originally planned to have the space ready by August... Lesson learned: don't count on someone else's construction schedule. That doesn't mean they are intentionally trying to mislead you, they could really be planning on having stuff ready by a certain date and be held back by the weather or something else beyond their control. Just be ready to hear a new deadline and plan a lot of buffer space for yourself.)

We wound up taking possession of the space a couple of days into October, but the real problem was getting our own "build-outs" done. What we received was a "white box": an empty shell. Basic electrical work, plumbing, etc. was all done but we had to put a floor in, paint, and do any other work. Luckily, for a retail business, our build-outs were pretty simple. We needed to paint, have a linoleum tile floor put down, and have our back room constructed. (The back room is where we have our kilns: the large ovens we fire pottery in.)

Unfortunately, it was a couple of weeks before our contractor could do the back room. We needed a wall put up and some mechanical and electrical work done before we could run our kilns. It wasn't until the very end of October and beginning of November that the work was scheduled to be done. This meant we could open, but we weren't going to be able to get anyone's finished pottery back to them.

Now we were *really* going to be cutting into our Christmas season. This wasn't making anyone very happy. So we decided to open up at half-capacity. Opening day was Saturday, October 12th, 2002.

Without the kilns running, we could have customers bead, look around, and book parties. We even let some lucky first customers paint some pottery for free that we would then use as samples in the studio.

Then someone (me, my partner... I don't remember who... it might have even been my mom), had a great idea. Why not let people paint pottery at a discount? We would just hang on to it a little longer than usual and when the kilns were up and running we'd fire it and call them to pick up.

It worked great! Customers painted at a 25% discount and we just had to do a good job of keeping track of all the pottery that was piling up. Some of our best and most frequent, regular customers started at that time and our first couple months turned out to be better than we expected.

The Good:
- We picked the right location.

The Bad:
- The landlord ultimately has control over my life and whether or not my business is able to make a profit.

Final Tidbits:

The landlord has a lot of control and power over your business. Know what you're signing before-hand. Ask as many questions as possible so you know what you're getting into. If you can afford it, use a lawyer not just to review the lease, but to help negotiate it. Location is supremely important to almost any business – but remember that the best locations typically demand the highest rents!

# Chapter 4
## Safe and Secure

It was one small burglary, but I felt it deserved it's own chapter because it's a good example of why any business owner needs to think about how to protect the business from any disaster that can happen when it's least expected.

When you start your own business, usually your funds are limited. You do your best to cut any corners you can. (We'll talk more about that in the chapter entitled "Money.") You're always asking yourself: do I *really* need to spend money on that?

I always planned to have a security system. It's a great tool for keeping track of employees coming and going. Each employee gets their own code number in addition to their store key. I'm able to tell who opened and closed the store and when. (And, if an employee leaves and "forgets" to bring back the key, I can simply delete them from the security system and not worry about it.)

But it got complicated when the security company gave me a huge list of op-tions. Do you want this sensor? Do you want the larger box? Do you want an extra button out here?

I wanted to keep it simple. I decided to save $100 bucks and only get a motion detector and not a motion detector and glass break sensor. I mean, if the glass gets broken, the motion will be detected, right?

And oh, I could have sworn they told me that things like balloons wouldn't set off the motion detector.

I got my first call from the security company about two hours after closing on a Saturday night, the first day of our Grand Opening party (which actually happened several months after we opened – more on that in Chapter 7). The motion sensor had gone off and they wanted to know if the police should be sent around. I said yes and was supposed to get a call back in a few minutes only if there was anything wrong. Since it was the first time I had been called, I couldn't wait those few minutes and wound up calling them back anyway to make sure nothing was wrong. Nothing was.

The next morning, my mom speculated that the balloons from our Grand Opening set off the alarm. I didn't think so because I thought they weren't supposed to.

The next night, after day two of our Grand Opening event, I got another call a few hours after closing time. I was a lot less panicked and this time we were sure it was the balloons.

New store policy: no balloons left overnight in the studio.

About a month later, I woke up in the middle of the night to the sound of my cell phone. (I should note that the security company knows to call my home phone first, and then my cell phone.) I answered it and it was one of my employees:

"Adeena, your store has been burglarized."

Now in that split second, the picture that I had in my head

was of all my pottery on the shelves smashed beyond recognition. I never thought I could be as awake and alert at 2 a.m. as I was then.

My employee went on to say that the cash drawer had been stolen, the pottery on the shelves was okay, that they had tried calling me almost a dozen times (I'm a heavy sleeper) and that I should talk to the officer who was there. My employee was super-upset and I was the one telling her that it would be okay, it could have been a lot worse. (Which is true, by the way.)

I'm not sure if I can describe the feeling of being in a hyper-alert semi-daze as the officer explained that a window was smashed, they took my cash drawer, and then described how they brought out a K-9 team to sniff around. I told the officer I'd be there in a half hour or less and he said he'd stick around until I got there.

My store manager was also there, and I talked to her briefly to make sure I could crash on her couch when this was all over.

So, I hopped into my Jeep and went down to the store. I can't tell you much about what was going through my head other than it probably was the quickest half-hour ride I ever drove. I think I was mostly concerned with not being pulled over for speeding on my way and having to explain…

Down at the store, one window pane out of 4 was smashed. My employee had left and it was just the officer and my store manager there. The officer took me through all the details.

The "perps" smashed the window with a baseball bat. How do they know a baseball bat was used? They left it. The police confiscated the bat and would check it for prints. The baddies ran off with the cash drawer and the police had to confiscate my receipt printer as evidence. There was a pile of glass on the floor just inside the store and the computer and monitor were tipped over but were not damaged.

There was a K-9 team involved and the officer explained how the dog tracked a scent down the road and then lost it. He said that was probably where the burglar(s) got into a car. After that he gave me his contact info and told me that there are 24-

hour window places listed in the phone book I could call to see about get-ting the window boarded up.

He also suggested that in the future, I do get the glass break sensor. Why? The cops are told by the security company what type of sensor was triggered and the officer said that they can take a little longer to reply to a "motion" sensor as opposed to a "glass break" sensor. He then reminded me about the false alarms they had been called to at my store just recently (those balloons, from the Grand Opening weekend).

The part I really had never thought about before this oc-curred was the 24-hour window place. The phone book only listed three or four 24-hour emergency window places. I called them all. Here's what I learned:

- Just because it says "24-hours," doesn't mean that's current information.
- Just because it says "24-hours," doesn't mean that someone will answer the phone.
- Just because they're listed in my local phone book, doesn't mean they'll respond to an emergency in my area. (We were a little too far for one of them to travel to in the middle of the night.)

(As a business owner and consumer, I wonder if this is considered false advertising…?)

I finally was able to contact the right company and they said that they would be out in a couple of hours to board up the window. Don't believe that part either. They wound up com-ing out to board up the window at about 9 a.m. the next morn-ing.

In the meantime, my manager and I stayed and wound up painting. Yes, painting pottery relieves stress. I can personally vouch for that.

All in all, it could have been a lot worse. I had to have a new cash drawer and receipt printer over-nighted. I lost less than $200 in cash from the drawer. My insurance covered most of the losses – the exceptions being what was in the cash drawer and my insurance deductible. (Cute Little Tidbit: When setting up insurance for a retail business, the money in the cash drawer isn't automatically covered. That's an additional option. Believing that most of my customers would not be paying in cash, I didn't opt for that and still don't. Most of our customers don't pay by cash and these days we never have more than $70 in the store overnight.)

We did open for business on time the next day. And the funniest thing is that most of the customers didn't even notice anything odd about the boarded up window until it was pointed out. Most of our conversations went like this:

Us to customer: "Hi, how are you today?"

Customer to us: "Oh, just fine, how are you?"

Us to customer: "Just fine considering, well, you know (pointing to boarded up window)"

Customer to us: "Huh? What's wrong?"

And then we'd explain what happened.

No, the police never did find out who did it. Yes, I have a glass break sensor in my store now and will have one in every store from now on.

About a year later, one of my regular customers asked me if they ever found the person who did it, and if it happened to be a particular individual who was just arrested for a local murder! She had read in the paper that when they caught him and searched his house, his basement was full of stuff that looked like it came from retail stores (my burglary was one in a series of retail burglaries over a couple months in my county – one not known for an overwhelming number of this type of crime). Who knows. It may or may not be. I'm past it now and much wiser.

(Another Cute Little Tidbit: Yes, we did have the security company's stickers on our windows. Whoever robbed us either didn't see them, or didn't believe them. I think too many small businesses put the stickers on their windows without really having the system, and most people just don't expect a small business to actually have an alarm system.)

Even if you didn't plan on installing a system (like I did because of the employees), I would still recommend it.

Imagine: your store is burglarized overnight and is sitting that way when you come in at 9 a.m. in the morning. Wouldn't that be awful?

The result of this burglary: I think something bad was bound to happen eventually. I just feel very lucky – if this was my bad thing, it wasn't *that* bad. I know another pottery studio owner who had a major flood, and another one who had a major fire. In both their cases, they were out of business for a while. Remember: I was open for business that day and no one was hurt.

The weird consequence: I had to change my cell phone ring. Every time I heard it, especially late in the evening, I'd get the SUPER uncomfortable feeling that something was wrong. That sound was now associated with something VERY BAD. The other thing is that for a while I became a very light sleeper and if my phone rang while I was in bed, I'd be up and sweating in an instant.

I know that at least one of you, while planning for your new business, has toyed with the idea of attempting to save money by foregoing insurance. Bad idea. Drop it right now.

Luckily, if you're in a retail location, the landlord will likely require in your lease that you have some form of property and/or business liability insurance.

The insurance paid for our replacement window and part of the new cash register equipment we needed.

The National Federation of Independent Business (NFIB), an advocacy organization for small and independent business, regularly publishes reports based on data collected from samples of small business employers across the country. In 2004, they published a report specifically on "Disaster." From this report, I learned that:

- 30% of small businesses were closed for 24 hours or longer due to a natural disaster. (This includes snow storms. I can relate – my store typically loses one or two days of business each year due to snow storms.)
- 10% experienced a man-made disaster. (Like my break-in.)
- 2-3% suffered an extreme impact. (Meaning that they were not operational for at least a week and/or had more than $100,000 in damages.)
- Whether or not the business had adequate insurance was most frequently associated with whether or not the business would continue operating.

It's important to note that this survey was published in 2004, before Katrina and the other hurricanes that ravished the Gulf coast in 2005. It is estimated that there were 900,000 small businesses in the affected area. The survey also pointed out that the percentage of businesses that closed for good due to a natural disaster is unknown because of the difficulty in tracking down owners afterwards. So that first statistic about the 30% of businesses that were closed for 24 hours or more only counts the businesses that re-opened after a natural disaster, not the ones that didn't. See the NFIB website (www.nfib.com) for more interesting reading material.

There are even some smaller things that not everyone thinks about. Sure, you have your birth certificate, the deed to your house and other important personal papers locked up somewhere that's fire- and water-proof... what about your important business papers?

After the Katrina disaster, magazines that write about small businesses were full of stories of business owners trying to rebuild their lives and businesses. I was amazed by how many stories I read in which the owners had kept all their important business papers (like their insurance policy!) in a plain file cabinet, with no backup.

I'll admit that for a while I didn't have a backup of some of my important papers, but I'm in the process of correcting that. I've actually gone a step further, and I recommend this to anyone who's not afraid of technology and spending even more time with their computer:

I bought Adobe Acrobat (www.adobe.com). This is the piece of software that makes those pdf files one is always downloading. My inkjet printer is also a scanner. So, I've been scanning my important papers and making them into pdf files. These files are easily searched, indexed, and smaller than if I saved them as some kind of image file. I'm saving all the important files to a CD and can make several copies of the CD to keep in different locations.

Here's a list of important business papers you should keep one or more backups of:

- Lease and other property related papers
- Insurance policies
- Tax returns
- Bank loan documents
- Any other agreements you've signed, or others have signed with you

And don't forget to have backups of any computer files that are important to your business!! This goes for any accounting software you use (keep a backup of your data someplace safe), Point of Sale software, and anything else!

Protecting against disaster in your personal life should also be a priority. What would happen if you wound up in the hospital? Or if something happened at your house and you were stuck there for a week. What if the worst happened and your spouse died?

Setting up a business that can run without you, having insurance, and even having a will: These are things you should do when starting your own Cute Little Store.

Donna Schreiter, who owns a store similar to mine called

The Painted Pot (www.thepaintedpotstl.com) in Chesterfield, MO, had to endure the unexpected loss of her husband of 24 years. If the emotional pain of this situation wasn't enough, she had to take over all the paperwork (taxes, payroll, accounting) and even install a new computer software system. Apparently, her husband wrote his own accounting software and without him, she had to start from scratch.

In addition, Donna's husband had another unrelated business with his family, and the proper paperwork wasn't in place to pass on his part of the ownership, rights and compensation to Donna, leaving her to figure out how to support herself and their kids.

It's important for anyone in business to have in place the proper paperwork to transfer ownership and assets if a spouse were to die. The law varies from state to state. This is one item that definitely requires the use of a lawyer and shouldn't be put off any longer than necessary.

There's a great book that I recommend over and over again: *The Small Business Owner's Guide to a Good Night's Sleep* See Appendix A for details.

So, to review:

The Good:
- Luckily, the burglary wasn't that bad and we were open for business the next morning.
- This is something that one can be reasonably prepared for (security system, insurance, etc.).

The Bad:
- No one wants to have to deal with this.
- We did lose money.
- Stress! Even after three years, I still always, always must have my cell phone on and always, always worry when it rings late at night.
- Owning a business like this means you are constantly at

risk for disaster: fire, flood, closing due to weather, accidents, illness. A lot of things can mean you're not open for business. You need to do your best to protect yourself against these happenings.

A Final Tidbit:
Prepare as well as you can. If you know what can happen, you can prepare for it.

# Chapter 5
## Employees

Not all businesses require employees. If you're a retail business, chances are you will want or need to have some – you can't be there seven days a week forever. Or maybe you can. However, business that wants to grow will almost certainly have to take on employees.

Recently, at a party, I spoke with a friend who owns a technology consulting business. He was complaining about not being able to take on some new business clients because he's already putting in sixteen-hour days. I made the obvious suggestion: "Why not hire someone to help you?" His response was something about how they might not do it right, or exactly the same way he would. "Yes, that's true," I said, but I reminded him that it is possible to train an employee in the important parts and if things aren't exactly the way he'd do it, that would be a trade-off.

I finished the conversation by asking: "How long are you going to keep working 16-hour days?" (I wanted to ask other questions like: Don't you want to grow your business?) He responded with that shrug of the shoulders that says, "Yeah, I know you're right, I can't keep this up forever," and we (okay, maybe it was just me) were promptly distracted by the hors d'oeuvers being carried by.

For a new (or any) retail business, there is an important trade-off: pay yourself or pay others to do work you are capable of doing.

If you choose the former option, you're running your store all the time or most of the time. Great! You're possibly saving hundreds to thousands of dollars on payroll. But if you're the one who has to be in your store the whole time, what other things are you missing out on? You might not have the time you'd like to do important things like marketing or attend networking events. You might not even be able to take time to go see a doctor.

However, you might choose to close your store when you're out. There are lots of small retail businesses that put the sign up "Out to Lunch" or close for a week when they're on vacation. That might be just dandy. But if you're in a shopping center like the one I'm in, you might be required by your landlord to be open a minimum number of hours, and possibly be required to be open seven days a week.

The downside of this "do-it-all-yourself" approach: presenting inconsistent hours to your customer can cause you to lose them. They think you're supposed to be open. When they show up and you're not, they will be annoyed. That means you've lost out on a sale right then, and possibly lost out in the future as well, since there's a good chance that the customer will find some other way or some other store to meet their needs.

(A Cute Little Tidbit from personal experience: We've

heard complaints about our nearest competitor being closed for several days during one of the local county school vacation weeks. Great for us! We picked up the extra business. On the not-so-good side, customers have been VERY quick to call and complain to us when we are supposed to be open at 10 a.m., and it's 10:10 and we're not open yet. This last part also goes under the heading of problem employees, discussed later in this chapter.)

So, for these reasons, we're going to assume in the rest of this chapter that a retail business needs employees and that you, as the prudent business owner, will opt to hire some quality folks.

When I opened The Pot & Bead I knew two things: 1) I needed employees, 2) I had to treat them well.

The Pot & Bead is open seven days a week. So unless I planned to be in the store EVERY SINGLE day without a break, I undoubtedly needed employees.

Yes, when we first opened, I was in the store every single day, but that only continued for about the first month or so. The first time I left my store while it was open, in the hands of an employee, it was very scary, but it was necessary. I think it was a lot like what it must feel like to leave your baby with a baby-sitter for the first time. (I don't have kids, so I'm just guessing at the comparison.)

Most of us have been an employee at one time or another. Every one of us probably has good and bad stories to tell. We have bosses we liked, ones we hated. That micro-managing, brow-beating, make-you-work-16-hours-while-your-child-is-being-born boss just might be the very reason you want to own your own business.

The last company I worked for before opening The Pot & Bead was marked by daily lessons in "how to *not* treat your employees." It was a pretty small company and the funny thing is that I initially wanted to work for that company because I believed that, at a small company, individual effort would be more frequently acknowledged and appreciated. Wow, was I wrong. Size does not matter.

For quite a while before I left, things had not been good. During this time I was racking my brain to figure a way to own my own company. The final straw, when I just knew it had to be done, was just after returning from a trip to Asia. I had been sent on this trip with a colleague with only two days notice. The purpose: convince our customer to not back out of their contract. In other words, we were sent to convince them to keep making their payments so we could keep operating.

We were successful (at least for the time being). But at a price (of course). My colleague and I both had gotten sick on this trip (I wound up with a nasty urinary tract infection and my colleague had other problems).

When we returned, not one of our managers or the people responsible for giving us this assignment said anything close to "Thank you" or "Good job." Instead, I was personally criticized for the work that wasn't able to be completed while we were gone. My colleague was denied reimbursement for his $60 or so of medical expenses. That would have been okay if the person denying them said something like: "You know that we're having some financial difficulties. We'd appreciate it if you'd cover this." But instead this person said something a lot more belligerent like: "What!? You think we're going to pay for that!? No way, you're crazy!" (Cute Little Tidbit: This isn't an exact quote. And the words weren't the most important thing. It was simply the tone and way it was handled.)

Well, that was the final straw. That was when all my free time went into thinking about how to get out of that kind of situation and into one where I had more control over my professional life.

It was only about three weeks later that I had my conversation with John over coffee that led to The Pot & Bead.

(I should note that being an employee wasn't all bad. Over the years I have worked for some wonderful people from whom I learned a lot, whom I respected a great deal, and who made a huge difference to my career.)

The good that comes from having been in those kinds of situations is that I had a very clear idea when I started this business of how I would and would not treat my employees. Knowing that your employees are valuable and need to be shown appreciation is key when you have them.

There are studies that show that the best (and possibly most profitable) retail businesses are ones that have the greatest employee satisfaction or those with the happiest employees. As an example, the grocery store Wegman's has made *Fortune* magazines list of top 100 companies to work for over most of the past decade. They've made the top 10 for the past four years. When they made #1 in 2005, *Fortune* published an article titled "The Wegman's Way" praising the company's way of treating employees and tying that atmosphere to the company's increasing market share.

Knowledge is indeed power, but it's not enough. Actually showing the appreciation is much harder than it would seem at first. Three years into this business, I think I'm better at it than before, but I'm still far from perfect.

Employees in a small, customer-service oriented business like mine have TREMENDOUS power. I don't think they even realize it.

A customer's perception of my store is directly tied to their first experience in it, which is directly tied to the experience they have with the staff member they first encounter. Therefore, if the employee provides good service, the customer will most likely come back and will hopefully tell people good things about my business. If the customer doesn't feel like they received good customer-service, they might not ever come back. What's worse is that they'll likely tell others never to come to my store.

So what do I want? Well-trained employees who like to work at The Pot & Bead. Who are these people? Well, in my ideal world they are all-knowing, with Einstein-level intelligence, are constantly beaming a genuine smile, have no other responsibilities besides working for me, are super punctual, can see the minutest of details, can juggle not two, not three but ten things at once, and love to clean.

Did I mention that my ideal world is that same magical fantasy land I dreamed up when I was six and thought I'd be living on the moon right now?

Back to reality on Earth, anyone who is going to be an employee of mine (or yours, for that matter) is a human being who, although they might be excellent, still isn't perfect and has a life and concerns outside of working in my store.

And really… what's to stop them from quitting and finding work someplace else?

I asked one of my high-school, part-time employees what she liked better about working at my shop versus the job she had prior at a bagel shop. She said she thought my place was more professional and more organized. This is some good feedback. Getting feedback from employees whenever you can is important, whether it's formal or not. Just the fact that you asked, and show genuine interest in their opinion, is what matters most.

Unfortunately, I don't have a magic recipe for finding and keeping the best employees. But after three plus years, I've been through my share of employees and have learned that the process we use to find and hire someone is one of the most important pieces of the puzzle.

First, we have a pretty detailed application and follow a thorough process for hiring someone (even for a part-time position). This involves reviewing the application, having the applicant come in for a 30-minute interview and making sure we call their references.

The two times I bypassed my own process and didn't do a good check of references but still hired the person are the only two times where I had to let those individuals go within a few weeks of their start date (and both times I wished I'd let them go a week sooner).

In order to truly work on and try to expand the business, I also knew early on that I would need a store manager. This is someone who is responsible for the other employees, and is responsible for the day-to-day flow of operations. In the latter case, a lot of the job revolves around making sure customers are happy and have their pottery returned to them on time.

I differentiate myself from my manager by this: My manager works "in the business." I work "on the business."

In the first three years, I went through four managers. I've learned something from each one. Employing a manager is different from employing part-time employees. The manager is often older and more experienced. This means that he/she demands more pay and benefits, like health care. You are competing with other employers to keep this person and often a small business doesn't have the resources to compete. (Home Depot or Lowe's can offer health care and a 401k, I can't.)

To keep all my employees informed and working like a team, we have a staff meeting every month. It's a time for some extra training, to make sure everyone knows the latest news at The Pot & Bead and for me to show my appreciation of them with the universal symbol: food.

To train, I usually give quizzes to the staff on topics that I want to make sure they really know. They know that there will be a quiz, and they know that it usually involves some kind of prize or incentive.

[Cute Little Tidbit: The meeting has also become a time for my staff to continue to harass me about having a baby in the near future (I keep assuring them that that's a couple years away at least!), or about my new boyfriend. The way I see it is this: If I can be a source of amusement to others, then I'm helping to make them happy and want to be around me and my business.

Employees do have their own lives outside of working for me (or you). You can take the attitude of, "So what?" and,

"What they do on their own time is their business" and, "As long as when they're on the clock, they're mine." But none of these approaches are particularly beneficial to the relationship.

Personally, I feel that any time an employee is not on the clock is none of my business and they can do whatever they like. However, I've had several employees take on second jobs and to date, it's never worked out well (for me). I've done my best to try to keep pay competitive and allow for the fact that different employees have different needs for numbers of hours worked. Scheduling each month usually takes a considerable amount of my time!

How do you really find and keep the best people? Like I said, I have no magic for this, but overall I think we've had more great employees than bad. And a couple of "okay" ones.

I have potential employees fill out a pretty detailed four page application. If I'm interested in them, they come in for a half hour interview. Once, after an interview with a potential employee, a customer who was painting in the store during the interview commented that he had never had such a thorough interview for any position. He's in sales with a salary in the six-figure range.

I look at it this way – it's my business. I'll do what I can to ensure that I'm hiring the best people possible. These people can make or break my business – I want only the best representing my business to my customers.

Here are some things I learned about the application process:

- The potential employee needs to pick up the application, fill it out him/herself and bring it back. Applications picked up and brought back by parents of high-schoolers tend to get ignored. It took hiring a couple not-so-great employees to realize that it was the parent who wanted their child to work, not the potential employee him/herself. (I know the parent is just trying to be helpful, but next time you're in a store and are receiving less-than-stellar service from the un-motivated youngin' behind the counter, ask yourself if this is this how you want your child to look and act in front of the public.)

- The application needs to be filled out completely! I've had applicants not sign the application, only put down half their address, put down the name of a reference without any contact information, and more. All this is a sign of someone who really doesn't care. If they don't care about taking the time to fill out their application, why would they care about taking the time to do their job properly? These applications find their way very quickly to the do not interview pile.

Then there's the interview. It typically lasts 15 to 30 minutes. Most of the applicants have worked before, so the questions are phrased in the form of: "What *did* you do in a previous situation?" as opposed to "What *would* you do if a situation happened?" This is called Behavioral Interviewing. The theory is that past actions indicate future behavior. The latter form of question asking doesn't give you any real information about the applicant because there is always a right answer to a question like: "If a customer came in upset, what would you do?" The applicant is usually smart enough to figure out the right answer to a question like this.

The question: "In your previous job, tell me about a time that a customer came in to complain. What did you do?" is much more likely to give you insight into how this person would handle a similar situation again.

(Important Little Tidbit: Before interviewing anyone for a position, make sure you're aware of the current rules and laws governing this process in your locality. You'd be surprised by the number of things you can't ask on the application or during the interview. Here's a few (this is not meant to be an all-inclusive list):

- Age (unless they are under 18)
- Race/ethnicity
- Sexual orientation
- "Family Status" (i.e., Are you pregnant? Are you planning to become pregnant?)

(You get the idea.)

Checking references is an important part of the application process. I do check references. The few times that I was lax in this area, it wound up biting me in the ass. Still, reference information does need to be taken with a grain of salt. After all, the applicant wouldn't write them down if he or she didn't at least believe that the reference would be positive. At least, I've never written one down without knowing that. If it's possible, ask the reference for other people to talk to.

But even after the application, interview and reference check, there is still no way to know if the person is going to work out. We also try to take into account the "first impression" the applicant has made with me and my staff. A person who presents his or her application with a big, genuine smile, speaks clearly and radiates enthusiasm is much more likely to do that with a customer than someone who drags their feet in, mumbles "herrrffssmuhappcation," makes no eye contact and leaves. (You can imagine that by now I have accumulated a very large "Do Not Interview" stack.)

(Cute Little Tidbit: If you've ever put in an application for a retail business and were never called, re-read the above few pages and make sure you're not making the same mistakes.)

As you may have gathered by now, it's very important that potential employees are friendly, up-beat, have a good attitude, and are responsible. But what about the pottery? Shouldn't they be artistic and artsy and know how to draw as well?

Nope. Not at all.

I can train someone how to work with our pottery. I can even teach them a few things about painting. I can't teach anyone about responsibility. (Even though we have a long training period, responsibility is learned over a life-time and, well, I just don't have that much time.)

Training someone to work at The Pot & Bead can take several weeks. This does cost money. I'm paying someone to learn, and usually need to pay at least a second person to be around to do the training, or I need to be there. It's a significant cost of doing business and something important to factor in. It should give you some motivation to make your business one that people want to work in and don't want to leave. "Turnover" as it's called, is expensive.

I don't care how cool it is to see Donald do it on *The Apprentice* (yes, I'm a fan, too), firing people ain't fun, but it is, unfortunately, necessary at times.

I think it does get a little easier the more times you do it because each time, you realize that you probably should have done it sooner. Eventually, it sets in that a bad employee can really hurt your business and you really can't afford to keep someone like that on your staff.

Here's a list of some of the things a bad employee can do to you and/or your business:

- lie
- steal
- be rude to customers
- not show up on time / not show up at all
- forget to do things
- quit unexpectedly and with no notice
- try to get fired
- call in sick with no notice
- close the store an hour early without permission

I've had employees do all of the above and more. The first

two are very difficult to prove, but if you suspect an employee of lying or stealing, you will wind up watching them like a hawk, and they'll wind up doing something else just as bad.

Being rude to customers can also be a little hard to prove unless a third person is around, but at the end of the day it's the customer's perception that's important. (See the chapter on Customers.)

Not showing up on time, especially when it means the store doesn't open on time, is unforgivable, but being late to any shift is grounds for being "written up."

Forgetting to do things, at first, doesn't sound too bad. Depending on your business, what kinds of things, and the frequency are all factors. For me, anything that gets forgotten that results in a disappointed customer is grounds for being written up. I had an employee forget to lock the store one night – that's grounds for a firing.

I've had at least one employee and one manager quit unexpectedly and with no notice. There's really nothing that can be done to prevent this, I believe. In the long run, it probably winds up hurting them more than me. (Word does go around, you know.)

And yes, I've had at least one employee *try* to get fired. I felt a little bad for her. I think she was under a lot of pressure at home and school at the same time and felt that if she quit, her parents would yell at her, but if she got fired, then she could tell her parents that I was the bad guy.

After almost two pages about the bad things employees can do, equal time and space belongs to the good.

The good things employees can do for you and your business:
- keep customers coming back
- have customers telling you how great you are for hiring such wonderful employees
- give you the freedom to go home
- take care of your business when you're sick and in the hospital

- allow you to go on vacation
- make suggestions for improvement
- allow you to work ON your business and not IN it

Just like the previous list, I've had all the above happen and more. Just after the store's two year anniversary, I wound up in the hospital unexpectedly for a week and in bed for the following two weeks. The happiest and saddest thing was when I realized that they really didn't need me in the store. And it was that same feeling and concept that allowed me to take a three week vacation overseas just after the store's third anniversary.

On any given day, here's the absolutely best thing that could happen to me: I'm out in the town someplace like the grocery store, someone I know (well or not-so-well) comes up to me and says "Hey Adeena! I was in your store with my child the other day. The person who was working there was great! He/She was so helpful, yada yada yada."

This almost exact conversation has happened more than once, and I look forward to it happening again. (The second best thing is when I'm working in the store and someone comes in to pick up their pottery and they say just about the same thing.)

This is a great place to bring up the concept of having procedures in place for your business. A business needs to have an operations manual.

It helps to set expectation levels with employees.

If you're not around, how do employees know what to do? Yes, you trained them, but what if they forget? What if your employee has worked for you for maybe three shifts and you're supposed to be at the store with them for shift #4. Unfortunately, you're stuck in traffic and are going to be late. But the store is still open and this new employee is the only one there. Oh, and lets say you're someplace where your cell phone doesn't get good reception either.

Luckily, nearly all your procedures are written down, and

on the first day the employee worked you let them know that the answers to almost all their questions are going to be in the manual.

So when a customer comes in and asks for X, the employee should know to check the manual – chances are the answer will be in there. (And if it's not, there's that procedure for handling things the employee doesn't know about – i.e., How to politely tell a customer that a manager or owner will need to get back to them about their question.)

I say that, chances are, the answer is in the manual. Your operations manual *is* a living document. Store policies, products and services will change over time so your manual will change over time.

I'm a very process-oriented person (largely due to my engineering background), so it was a very natural thing for me to start writing our operations manual. I did most of it in the few weeks before we opened. I didn't get all of it from the top of my head. A ceramic studio trade association I belong to provided some resources as did other books on retail.

After The Pot & Bead opened, there were lots of little tweaks to the manual in the first few months. About a year after opening, I did a major re-organization of it to help with training new employees. Every year I look at it to see what needs updating.

Communication between myself and the employees is another area that always requires thought and work. There is always some tidbit or customer service note to pass on to and between employees. What if one of our policies changed? What if a customer had a special request for her upcoming birthday party?

We've tried several approaches to make sure everyone who works at The Pot & Bead is on the same page. What started out as a sticky-note system has evolved into using an internet-based web service that allows us to communicate whether or not we're physically in the store.

Forms, logs, and contracts are also things we use between ourselves and our customers to keep it all straight. (Cute Little Tidbit: Not all commercial printers are created equal. Some specialize in creating forms – printing up a two or three part form where you write on the top page and it's carbon copied to the bottom page(s) – so we can have a copy as well as the customer.)

Keeping good employees around is another challenge. You have a great employee – one who always is there on time, knows what to do, and is great with customers. This person is great and you really want him or her to stay forever and be happy working in your business.

But then one day they come to you. They've found another job. It pays more.

Urgh! First, you didn't know that this employee even was having an issue with her pay. Why didn't she at least say something?

What do you do? Well, I have to say, that unfortunately, there have been a couple times that I've lost good employees because I couldn't afford to pay them more at the time.

The best I could do is re-evaluate what I was paying for the type of job versus other local businesses. When we first opened, I thought I was paying competitively. But I expect a lot from my employees – they aren't there to just ring the cash register. They need to do everything from answer the customers' questions about painting, to taking care of their pottery, to running birthday parties. Our base pay is more now, but I also won't settle for an employee who isn't representing The Pot & Bead in the way I want.

(Cute Little Tidbit: As a way to improve employees pay, we give a bonus at the end of the month that's based purely on the store's sales. Each month there is a sales target the store has to meet. How much does each employee get? A percentage based on the number of hours they worked. The idea is, the more they worked, the more they would have contributed to overall sales that month.)

But my learning how to pay people has cost me some good employees. The problem, however, isn't just the pay. It's the fact that I didn't know the particular employees were unhappy with what they were making. I really didn't know that they were already looking for another job. I found out after they had found another job, accepted it, and given me their Two Week's Notice.

The real problem was that the employee didn't feel comfortable coming to talk to me about this ahead of time. Unfortunately, this was my problem – I'm not the most approachable person on the planet. In any employment situation, I believe there's a little natural animosity towards "The Boss." "The Boss" is the bad person who makes you work and controls a big part of your life. Couple that with the perception that "The Boss" will yell and scream and get mad if you come ask for a raise, and it makes people think it's easier to quit rather than ask.

(Cute Little Tidbit: I have never "yelled" at an employee. Yes, I have been mad and even upset, but yelling doesn't do any good. If an employee is doing something bad enough that would make me want to yell, then this person shouldn't be my employee.)

(Tidbit for employees: If you're unhappy with your job, whether it is pay or working conditions or anything else, go to your boss and ask, "Can we talk?" I think most employers are more approachable than people think. Unless you've talked to them about your issues specifically before, they probably have no clue that you have issues. That doesn't mean that your employer can change anything to help make you happier, but at least you'll be able to honestly say you tried when you give up and go find another job.)

(Tidbits for folks contemplating owning or who already own their Cute Little Store: Are your employees happy? What are their big issues? It might not even be with you, it might be in their lives at home, but do you know about them? Do your best to get to know these people who help keep your business running. It's hard, and when you ask questions like: "How are you?" you might get the generic "I'm fine" response, but keep at it.)

So your employees might not tell you everything going on in their lives. That's okay, you're not entitled to that information. But you are entitled to know what's going on in your store when you're not there.

I had an employee who was very nice and pleasant with the customers, but we were starting to have issues because she wasn't getting all the tasks done that she was supposed to when she was there by herself. It was strange because she was not the irresponsible type – she wouldn't blow off work just to blow it off. After working with her some more, we realized that she couldn't multi-task. For example, if she was helping a customer on the phone and a customer walked into the store, she had to finish with the customer on the phone before helping (or even at least acknowledging) the customer in the store.

Or when a customer was in the store painting, she couldn't do another task once the customer was set up and painting – she had to sort of hover over this customer. (Our normal mode of operation is once a customer is set up, we give them their space and go off to do another task, while checking on them occasionally and making sure we're available to answer any questions.)

This person's employment came to a quick end when two things happened. First, her *husband* called in sick for her the night before she was supposed to open the store on her own the next morning. Apparently, she had been sick the whole weekend, but for some reason, they waited until the last minute to call, when it was impossible to get someone to take her shift. Two things wrong here: 1) waiting until the last minute when, if she was sick all weekend, she could have called much sooner, and 2) having her husband call in for her. We only deal with employees – if someone else is calling, then the person should be in the hospital or something really bad like that. I am convinced that this employee wasn't sick, but stressed about coming in to the shop the next day and had her husband call because she didn't want to tell me herself.

The second thing was when I found out that same day that a *customer* had helped take care of other customers because too many things were going on at once for this employee to handle. I was floored. Why didn't she (the employee) say something?

The day before this happened, I had had a discussion with the employee about the tasks she was supposed to accomplish the next day. It was going to be the first time she would load a kiln full of pottery on her own. Every employee has to do this on their own at some point. I worried that this was a little too soon for her, and we discussed other options: the task could wait or I could come in and do it. She maintained that she could do it, no problem.

Well, apparently, it was too much to get it done and take care of customers. She was upset that she couldn't get it done *and* take care of customers. She didn't know how to manage both. When I found this all out, I knew I had to let her go. Being able to multi-task to some degree is definitely a job requirement in a small business.

The balance of being involved in the day-to-day operations of your business versus empowering employees to deal with things without you is a fine line that constantly needs monitoring and adjusting.

Find out what decisions your employees made and validate them or let them know what to do in the future. Remember that you can't plan for everything that comes up, but you can plan for a lot and be ready to add a store procedure or policy when something new happens.

The only decisions that employees make on their own that truly make me upset are ones that would make us lose customers or business. I feel a wonderful sense of accomplishment and appreciation when an employee is able to make a decision without me and it turns out to be exactly the same one I would have made.

The Good:
- Good employees are one of the best assets you can have as a business owner.  Good people are out there – find them!

The Bad:
- Bad employees can really hurt your business.  Get rid of them quickly.

Final Tidbits:
Only you can decide if, when, and how many employees are right for your business.  I am a firm believer that in the long run, any business that intends to grow can't just be made up of the owner or founder.  Every growing business will need to experience the joy and pain of employees.

# Chapter 6
## Follow Your Gut

The plan from Day 1: If The Pot & Bead is successful and proves that it has the potential to turn a profit, we'll open more stores like it!

This was more than just a thought. A few months after opening, I had my accountant prepare financial projections for multiple stores within a few years.

At the start of our first summer (The Pot & Bead had been open for less than a year), a store similar to mine went on the market. They were going to have to sell or close. Quickly. This is all the information I received in an email one day. This other store was also within driving distance of my house.

It turned out that the owner was terminally ill.

I looked into it, and at first, it looked like a good idea. The store had been open for about four years and was marginally profitable in the previous full calendar year. The current calendar year wasn't going so well. Because the owner had been ill since January, there had been virtually no advertising or marketing done that year. Also, the owner was the store manager... he worked both *in* and *on* his business.

Somehow I saw huge potential. But by the tone I'm using now, you might be able to guess: pursuing this "opportunity" proved to be a huge mistake.

The goal on both sides was to make this a simple, non-costly process. Mistake #1 was when I thought we could avoid using a lawyer in the process. I mean, there are all these books out there with titles such as *Legal Forms for Small Businesses*. These books typically include standard contracts for selling a business. We had agreed via email what the terms would be and agreed that these documents would be okay. I snagged one from just such a book, added in our specific arrangements and it looked like we had a deal.

Some of the details of the deal were that I would be giving the sellers a down payment and the rest of the purchase price would be seller financed. This meant that I'd be making payments to them over a period of time at some interest rate – effectively, they're granting me a loan. As such, they wanted something to act as collateral for that loan. They initially asked to put a lien on my house.

(Important Tidbit that will come up later: When they asked for the lien on the house, my now ex-husband and I thought to ourselves that that was strange considering we have absolutely no equity in the house. Meaning: we're young (we haven't had years to build up much equity), we have our first mortgage, our home equity loan, and the business loan that started The Pot & Bead. We assumed that the sellers didn't actually expect us to have any equity in our home and that they were asking just to show something on paper. In other words: the sellers didn't ask us how much equity was in our home and we didn't tell them. They asked for the lien, we shrugged our shoulders and said "sure.")

The sale was supposed to be executed on August 1st of that year. The sellers were unable or unwilling to keep the store open past July 31st. The value of a retail business plummets when the store is actually closed, so it was in my best interest to make sure it stayed open past then.

The problems started when we discovered that the sellers were going to be out of town for a few days before and a few days after our execute date. Well, since it seemed like we had an agreement, we agreed that as of August 1st, I'd start running the business and we'd sign the agreement when they returned. Sounds simple and reasonable, right?

One thing led to another and the agreement didn't get signed. My husband and I were trying to re-finance our house (more on all these money problems in the chapter on Money) and that held up some of the paper work getting this other lien for the sellers on our house. It wasn't until the end of August, with the lien paperwork started, that the sellers actually saw that we had three liens already and that's when it dawned on them that we didn't actually have any equity in our home. They didn't like that and called me back and asked me to produce some other form of security for this loan. I think I laughed. I didn't have anything else. We went back and forth on this for a while. They kept asking, and I kept saying I didn't have anything. They asked about my parents and using their homes. Not a bad idea, but my parents have their own financial issues and couldn't afford to get involved in mine.

Eventually, they gave in, probably because they saw the deal falling through if it didn't happen this way. It was a risk they had to take.

By then it was September and I was starting to have second thoughts about the whole deal. That was the time that I should have started listening to my gut. I should have cut my losses then. Actually, when we started the whole nonsense about extra security for the loan something in my gut told me then to can the deal, but I didn't. I should have.

But no… I let it go on through late October. Right through

our Grand Re-Opening. It was actually at the Grand Re-Opening when it finally set in that I should get out of this deal. I realized that the type of customer in this area was not the kind of customer that I understood. I had to get out of this deal.

Luckily, something happened the next week that made it all the easier. The sellers emailed me an agreement document that was completely different from the one we had actually agreed to at the beginning – they changed the agreement at the very last moment without my knowledge. So that was it. We said no.

For a long while afterwards, I would tell people that I felt bad about the whole thing and people would tell me, "Don't. It's business." And they're right.

I spent the next several months depressed over the money that I was out. I was out about $15k. (Operating the business cost more than it was bringing in at the time; I spent money on new marketing materials and advertising.)

I have to confess that what made me finally feel better was the following: The sellers did manage to sell the place to someone else. The following January, I got a call from the new buyer who was in a state of panic and despair herself. She bought the business thinking that 1) she'd be able to take a salary, and 2) that she'd be able to spend MORE time with her 10-year-old.

She said she was nervous about calling me because the sellers had said many bad things about me. I told her I wasn't surprised by that given what had happened and told her my side of it. She wanted to know how sales were when I managed that shop and if I could recommend any things she could do. She told me how surprised she was that she was not able to spend more time with her daughter and the despair she was in over not being able to draw a salary.

(Cute Little Tidbit: This is actually one of the main reasons I wrote this book – it's to help prevent people from making the mistake this woman did. She thought owning her own

Cute Little Store would mean more time and money. This is *exactly* the mistake I want to prevent others from making.)

I told her about sales during the time I ran the store and how they weren't covering expenses. I told her how much money I was out. I let her know what the sales were and what expenses were.

She was upset because she had told the sellers that she expected and needed to draw a salary from the business and was very upset that the sellers knew it wasn't realistic and didn't say anything. Well, it's business. Even though it would have been nice for them to say something, they didn't have to. Their motivation was to sell the business. They didn't care what they were sticking someone with.

But the seller didn't conceal any information, they actually didn't do anything wrong. It was the buyer's mistake. This buyer did not practice the concept of due-diligence. It's where a potential buyer of a business researches the business in detail, by looking through all the financials and any other information. This step typically occurs after the potential buyer enters into some form of agreement, and possibly has even put down some earnest money (it's serious buyers, not just anyone who asks, who can have access to this privileged information). If you're contemplating buying a Cute Little Store, read at least one of the books in Appendix A which discusses buying a business.

In this case, the buyer should have had access to the sales and expense data from the previous owner. Even with a cursory glance at the financials, she would have seen that the previous owner didn't draw much of anything resembling a salary.

The good that came from this was that it probably prevented me from making a more costly mistake later. Businesses go up for sale all the time. Towards the end of that deal, another paint-you-own-pottery business was up for sale. This one had been profitable a while ago and was currently on its second owner, who had let the business deteriorate. Even though a part of me wanted that business pretty badly, my gut was definitely saying no; and this time I listened.

A retail consultant who I used for a while early on who is also the author of *The Profitable Retailer*, Doug Fleener, once asked me: Is it a "nice-to-have" or is it something that can return a profit? That's a question I now ask myself every single time I'm considering opening my checkbook.

I think I get it now. "Nice-to-haves" are the things you want. They might make you feel better about yourself. But if something is a "nice-to-have," hopefully your gut will be telling you "No."

How do you recognize that? If you listen to your inner voice, you'll notice that there is a conflict. In my case, I get some stress symptoms popping up. Yes, your "gut" isn't just something metaphorical, I believe it really exists and will manifest itself in different ways for different people. Learn to follow it.

The Good:
- Another mantra I like to chant to myself (or others when I hear them complain): "It could have been worse!"
- It was a good, albeit expensive, learning experience.

The Bad:
- I really didn't have that money to lose back then. It took over two years to recover from that loss. Since I didn't have the money to lose, it had to come from someplace. It meant that I had problems paying for other things and had no reserve when a real emergency came up.
- The stress.

A Final Tidbit:
In any situation like this, you need to use a lawyer! You cannot let your emotions affect what you know are sound business decisions – even if that means you'll be perceived as "not nice." Simply put: follow your gut

.

# Chapter 7
## Customers… Ya Gotta Love Them

I love my customers. They give me money. What's not to love about that?

Seriously.

Retail is all about customer service. Yes, my customers like painting pottery too. But pottery painting isn't a necessity. If they didn't enjoy the whole experience, they could easily find another way to spend their entertainment dollars.

I was at a business seminar once, and during the introduction the speaker asked the people in the audience to raise their hand if they were in a customer service business. I thought he was looking to differentiate between businesses that "sell a service," like accounting, but it turned out I just sat there for the next few minutes feeling embarrassed that I didn't raise my hand.

I am indeed in the customer service business (I say this now, after just a few chapters ago trying to convince you I was in the retail business.)

Those two terms, "retail" and "customer service," should really be interchangeable. Retail is about selling a product to an end user. But customer service is what will make that customer come back, remain loyal, and bring her friends and family.

Did you know that there are businesses out there turning away customers? This seems to be a new trend with retail stores – there are customers out there that suck the life out of you. They will browse and ask many questions but in the end, never buy anything. These retail businesses are implementing the 80/20 rule. 80% of their business comes from 20% of their customers and they are trying to cut out some of the non-profitable ones.

While I'm not comfortable actually doing that, I am indeed a believer in the 80/20 rule. In fact, just before our two-year anniversary, I analyzed our sales data and found it to be true. Nearly 80% of our business came from 20% of our customers.

First, I want to SUPER thank that 20%. You are great. You are wonderful. Please keep giving me money.

Showing customers you value them is just as important as appreciating your employees. Without them, business would not be good. Customer appreciation is another one in the long list of on-going activities that the Cute Little Store owner must fret over.

So for our second anniversary, instead of having a generic "Anniversary Sale," we sent some free offers to those customers. We divided our top tier of customers into two groups: the best and the VERY best. We sent out invitations to our top customers and their families to come paint special mugs for themselves... completely free – no strings attached. Most of them did this. It was a pure thank you.

I'm waiting for our 5th anniversary to have a big blowout

party. In the meantime, we've done some smaller scale things (like what was mentioned above) to reward customers.

Are all of our customers wonderful? No. Some can be downright mean. No, they're not really mean but a lot of times it can come out that way simply because their expectations aren't being met.

I've been told to think of these customers not as "mean," but as "unhappy." The premise is that you can't make a mean customer nice, but you *can* make an unhappy customer happy. (Trying to have some of the younger employees implement that way of thinking is what's really hard.)

Before you can make customers happy, before you can appreciate them, you need to know who they are. Do you know who your customers are?

Collecting data and customer feedback is an important activity for the business owner.

Okay, it might be my geeky science background, but I'm all about collecting the data. When customers are in the store, we do ask them for their address and email address. We also ask them how they first heard about us.

Our "Point of Sale" software (cash register software) allows us to keep customer data like phone numbers and addresses with the customer. It also keeps a record of the customer sales history so I can go back and see all of the customers who bought a toothbrush holder in 2003.

To gather feedback, once a year, we mail out a customer survey. Each year the survey changes based on areas of the business I'm looking to most improve.

I also give out mini-surveys at the end of programs like the Summer Camp that we run.

I will also flat out ask customers specific questions for feedback on specific areas.

What do I do with all this information? It makes it easier to decide where to spend my advertising dollars, who to market

to, *what* to market, how to improve customer service, etc.
Information from customers is vital.

If you're a business owner, you're still a customer to someone else. Lots of consumer magazines tell us to ask for discounts, lower rates, etc. But then when we're the business owner, we're on the receiving end of everyone else asking for special treatment and discounts.

Many customers ask for a special discount because they think they've been to the store a lot. Others just ask. I had a five year old boy ask me out of the blue if I could give him anything for free.

Most of us grew up with the phrase "the customer is always right" tattooed on our brains. Well, that's not exactly true. Customers are wrong all the time. They get information mixed up, or are simply the victims of miscommunication. It's our job to figure out what they really want, what they're saying, and send them home happy.

Keeping the customer happy is one of the hardest things to do. You have to be prepared to set and meet customers' expectations.

Watch *Seinfeld*. Practically every other episode has a significant amount of time devoted to some crappy customer service issue with a retail store or restaurant. Can you picture a retailer really acting like that today? I can't. Service is king, and knowing that is half the battle. If you know and understand the reasons why good customer service rules, you can act on that information. It should be easy, but for some reason that's one of the hardest things ever (right up there with employee appreciation).

Doug Fleener, who wrote *The Profitable Retailer*, believes you should never say "No" to a customer. Nice thought, but is it possible to live up to? Employees need to be trained on when and how they can say "Yes" when a customer asks for something unusual.

Here's a funny, but true, story:

A friend of mine and her husband were out for a special Valentine's Day dinner. They were at a pretty nice steak and seafood restaurant – one where a dinner for two will cost you at least $100.

After checking out the menu, my friend realized that they had a special with two lobster tails and other meals with steak, but no "surf & turf" meal. She asked the waiter if she could have one lobster tail and a steak.

As she told me the story the day after, I was thinking to myself that the waiter should have instantly said "Yes" to this request, but I knew that's not where this was going. She went on to describe how the waiter had to talk to the head waiter, who came over to verify the request before holding a conference of waiters, cooks and staff employees in the back. Who knew that asking to put two pieces of food (that the restaurant already had on the menu) on the same plate would cause such a commotion?

Luckily, my friend did get her "surf & turf" meal and has a great sense of humor and can laugh about the whole thing.

Customer service is about training your employees to know when to follow your policies and procedures, but also about training them to know when they can veer from the norm and say "Yes" to make a customer happy.

...and then you have to have a thick skin. No matter how hard you try, you can't please everyone. There will be that random customer that isn't happy and you have to let it go. She/He might say something nasty. You have to let that roll off your back and move on.

If you've tried your best and couldn't please someone, learn from that experience, keep a positive attitude and move on to the next customer, whom you *will* make happy!

Keeping customers informed is the other big challenge for a small business. Let's say you have a new product or are offering a new service. How do your customers know about it?

In my dream world, we would telepathically send news to customers while they were sleeping. They would wake up each morning thinking of The Pot & Bead and know all about what was happening at the shop that day. Aaaaahhhh.... I wish.

A little closer to reality... we could call each customer and let them know our news. This isn't far fetched for a lot of businesses. This kind of marketing to existing customers can pay off.

But our customer database contains thousands of names, addresses and phone numbers. We need something a little more practical to keep our customers informed.

Practical *and* economical. Remember that every time I open my checkbook, I'm thinking about what the dollars I spend are going to go out and do for me. (See the chapter on Marketing and Advertising for more details on how to spend and not spend those dollars.)

The thought I want to leave you with here is that keeping customers informed is important, and a challenge.

Lastly, remember that you're a customer, too. Every time you walk into some else's store, Cute or otherwise, take note of your experience there. Here are some things I look for:

- Was I acknowledged by an employee? How well?
- If I have a question, how easy is it to get an answer?

Since owning my own store, I try to be more patient on long lines and when I'm patronizing another store that's busy. I also like to pay attention to other people's problems. Is the woman in line in front of me yelling at the young girl behind the counter? Why? How is the employee handling it? What could have been done to prevent it?

When this happens, I try to be reassuring to the employee behind the counter. Most times when I've seen a situation like this, the employee was just used as a verbal punching bag by the disappointed customer. Whatever made the customer unhappy probably wasn't this particular employee's fault, but the customer was too angry or disappointed to be polite or to care.

The lesson that I take back to my own store is that I don't want my employees to be used as verbal punching bags. I try to empower my employees to handle the situation – to be able to do something to make this customer happy.

Usually it works, and usually we have happy customers. And when customers tell me they're happy… well, that just makes my day.

The Good:
- Customers give you money – this is why you're here, this is why you're in business, and what will keep you in business.

The Bad:
- Some customers demand A LOT more for that money than you can give them.

Final Tidbits:

Do your best to take care of your customers and they will take care of you. As a fellow Cute Store Owner, I can tell you that you're not perfect and you never will be and that when you encounter a customer service issue, resolve it quickly, make the customer as happy as you can and move on. The negativity from the situation can drag you down – don't let it. Think about those wonderful, great customers who are keeping you in business.

# Chapter 8
## Competition

About a month or so before we opened I found out that a store similar to my own would be opening five minutes away. Typically, mine is the kind of business where you only have one per town, not two. Someone else was going to try and take money from my customers.

I commiserated with other paint-your-own-pottery studio owners I knew across the country. They tried to put me at ease by telling me: "Adeena, what's going to happen is that people in your town will go to both locations, and then go back to the one they like the best."

Translation: We had to be the best. This really meant that we would have to have superior customer service every day.

Soon after we opened, lots of folks would come into my shop and say things like: "Weird, there's another studio like this over in that other shopping center." They would all ask me: "Are you two affiliated? Owned by the same person?"

And what still makes me feel good is that they would sit there and tell me all the differences between the two studios and why they like mine better. Even after three years, I still get folks saying nicer things about us in comparison.

Another NFIB survey on competition reports that almost half of all small business owners' main competitors are located within ten miles of their business. On the other hand, small business owners operate in highly competitive environments and compete against small and large firms, large chain or box stores, and that competition can be located anywhere on the globe.

This means that in your Cute Little Store, you need to be thinking about the quality of customer service you offer and the quality of your product. These are the two major ways that small businesses are able to compete.

One thing I make sure to do is to never bad-mouth the competition myself. If a customer starts putting the competition down, I listen politely, but I don't chime in. When I'm asked if we're affiliated, I politely say no, it was just a coincidence that we opened at similar times, in close proximity.

If people ask me if we're alike (when they've heard of the other place, but haven't been there), I politely point out our differences. But of course, I don't say anything bad about the competition. We stay positive and focused on who we are, and I train my employees to follow my lead in this area.

Occasionally, a customer might say something good about the competition. It's very hard to hear. (It's like hearing your boyfriend or spouse tell you that his ex was great at something.) But you must resist the temptation to instantly point out one of their flaws in retribution. That's simply too negative. Just smile and nod politely. I mean, the customer is telling you what they think or feel from her own perspective – you don't want to be the person to invalidate that. It might be appropriate to point out what you do that's positive and similar. You might even wind up learning something about how to improve your business.

There is, however, more competition than just the other paint-your-own-pottery shops around. A main source of our business is birthday parties. Well, this means that everyone else who offers birthday parties is also my competition. This includes the local bowling alley, skating rink, pool, and even many local restaurants.

Like I said at the beginning of the chapter, anyone who takes money from my customers is my competition. I'm in competition will all other forms of entertainment to be the activity the customer chooses.

How do you compete? What makes you different? What makes you better? These are all questions you have to ask yourself and be prepared to answer. Then, every year or every few months you need to go back and do the same thing again. (There are lots of books on business that cover this in what is called a "S.W.O.T." analysis: looking at your Strengths, Weaknesses, Opportunities, and Threats. See Appendix A.)

What are your differentiators? In a retail business, they can be anything from location to the products you offer.

In a retail business like mine, the thing that will make the biggest difference is customer service. Customers want service. They don't want to be ignored, or treated badly. They want to be acknowledged. They want their questions answered and their expectations met.

Another thing that sets us apart is price. Our prices are generally lower than our competition, but we don't compete on price alone. Although it should be obvious – lower price is (almost) always a better differentiator for a customer. Beware of lowering prices *just* to beat the competition; beware of being labeled as a "you get what you pay for" type of business.

Product is another differentiator. Do you offer products

your customer wants? We frequently respond to customers who say "I wish you had..." by expanding our offerings if and when it's possible. We want customers to know that we have the products they want.

Other things that might differentiate your business: hours, policies, truly unique products and services, etc.

At the end of the day, you need to be able to clearly and concisely say and know what sets you apart from your competition.

In order to do that, one of the things you need to be aware of is what the competition is doing and how it may affect your business.

First, understand who your competition is. (Remember from above that it's not just the obvious.) In the county where my store is located, there are three other paint-your-own-pottery stores currently in operation. Then there are all the other places that do birthday parties – it seems like everyone offers birthday parties for kids. Make a list. Better yet, make a spreadsheet which you can update regularly.

In order to understand what your competition is doing, it's research time. The easiest way to begin this research process is to look at their websites. I look for the following information and add it to my spreadsheet:

1. address and phone number
2. hours
3. main products and/or services
4. pricing (pick a sample product or two)
5. years in business

This is just the start. Next, if it's at all possible to visit the business, then that's what ya gotta do. If you're like me, and feel a little weird walking right into the territory of the enemy, then send a proxy.

I frequently send family, friends, and employees to "spy" on the competition. In the case of looking at other paint-your-own-pottery stores, I give them very specific instructions about what I'm looking for. They don't just go in, look around a little and leave. They go in, pick a piece, paint it, store some information in their head, and then leave.

(Important Little Tidbit: If you're not in business yet, research on your potential competition is very important and should be included in your business plan. This is especially true if you're seeking financing. One of the things a potential lender wants to see is if you know and understand your competition – only by understanding them can you compete.)

Competition gives me a weird feeling in the gut. I have to admit a little secret here: I really don't like confrontation. So every time I come face-to-face with competition or something similar, I get a little shaky and am looking for the nearest rock to hide under.

That's one of the many stressful things we all have to deal with. We deal, and then move on.

The Good:
- Competition forces you to be better.

The Bad:
- There will always be other businesses and people out there competing for your customers' dollars, no matter what you do.

A Final Tidbit:
Put on your thick skin, get in there and compete. Be ready to offer higher quality and better service than your competition.

# Chapter 9
## They Gotta Know You're There

Marketing is getting people to know about your business and convincing them to come in and give you money.

I consider advertising to be a subset of marketing. It's the marketing you pay for.

Marketing is one of my largest sources of stress, yet it is also, for me, one of the most personally rewarding parts of owning this retail business.

It's stressful because you ALWAYS need to think about it. Its great that this month might be a good month, and sales are high, but good sales this month doesn't necessarily have anything to do with sales next month or the month after. We need to think now about getting customers in the door in the future.

But I say it's rewarding because 1) it allows me to show

my creative side, 2) some marketing events and activities can be directly tied to sales, which is rewarding, and 3) some marketing events generate immediate praise from the people who see them. (Receiving praise is almost as good as receiving money after all the hard work you've put into an event.)

It's important to do your best to track marketing events to results. You want to know what worked and what didn't. Here is a list of things we've done. (Cute Little Tidbit: WWFMMNWFY – What Works For Me May Not Work For You!)

Grand Opening
- What: A few months after we opened, we held the official event where we invited our existing customers to come paint a tile that we would use to decorate one of the walls of our studio. It was completely free, no obligation to buy anything, but we did have a sale for those who wanted to.
- How well it worked: Really well! We wound up with over 300 tiles for our wall and had decent gross sales that weekend, too, since most people who painted a tile de-cided to also paint something else.
- How much effort: Ahead of time, we created and mailed out invitations, arranged to have a helium tank around for balloons, and ordered food. The two days of the event were a lot of work since we had nearly a full store all day, both days. Afterwards, we had the task of glazing and firing all 300 tiles, then putting them up on our wall.
- Variations: There's not much I would have changed about this event. It went really well. Years later, people still come into the store to see their tile on the wall. It's had the additional affect of making us part of the community.

Survey Mailing
- What: We sent out a single page, double-sided survey to exist-ing customers in the mail. If they filled out the survey and bought it back in, they would get $1 off. Each year we did this, the theme of the survey was dif-ferent (i.e., one year we were interested mostly in birth-day parties).
- How well it worked: The first year, it worked well in the sense that I expected to get 1% of them back and we got a little more than that. I had worked out that if 1% of those we sent it to brought it back and used the cou-pon to paint in the store, it would have paid for itself. The 2nd year we did this, although we got a lot of them back, the mailing was larger (more people after two years) and it didn't pay for itself.
- How much effort: I had to design the survey and the mailing, then have it printed and mailed. The effort seems to be worth it, the cost is not. Several hours can be spent afterwards tallying the results.
- Variations: We still do surveys, but not in the mail any-more. We have transitioned to using an online survey maker that gets emailed to our customers. It's much more cost effective, and the results are tallied for you.

Email Newsletter
- What: We send out a newsletter via email approxi-mately twice a month.
- How well it works: I think this is one of the best, most cost-effective marketing efforts we employ. We collect customers' email addresses when they come in to the store and add them to the mailing list. They always have the option of removing themselves and I have re-ceived lots of positive feedback from customers who say they enjoy receiving and reading our newsletter.
- How much effort: It takes quite a bit of creativity to keep this fresh and interesting. It's a good thing that I

like to write.

Attending local marketing events

- What:  In the county where my business is located, we have a very active Chamber of Commerce that hosts several events throughout the year that are opportunities for small businesses to market themselves.
- How well it works:  These events give me the opportunity to make one-on-one contact with other people who can become customers in my store and several have.
- How much effort:  That depends on our involvement in the event itself.  Some events I just attend and hand out my business card and flyer.  At another event, we were the "key sponsor" and took that opportunity to get the other 150 attendees to do some paint-your-own-pottery right there.  (Typically the key sponsor gives a 15-20 minute speech.)  This event required a lot of preparation on our part ahead of time, but we gained several new customers and  stood out in the Chamber in a different, positive, and certainly memorable way.

One of the misconceptions of retail that I want to de-bunk right here: the "build-it-and-they-will-come" theory.  This theory doesn't work in retail.  And when it occasionally seems like it does work, it's usually a temporary effect.

Marketing is constant.  Marketing doesn't go away.  You always need to be thinking of how to bring customers in the door.  Bringing customers inside is one of the hardest things a retailer has to do.

The Pot & Bead opened right at the beginning of the holiday season:  mid-October 2002.  We had an AMAZING holiday season.  It surpassed all my projections.

We had done some marketing, but some of the best marketing had been done for us before we opened.  We were in a brand new building, in the center of our community.  So for the first year, there was a lot of natural curiosity by people who had driven by the shopping center for months wondering what was coming. There was a lot of anticipation and build-up that we benefited from. But that was just the first year.

A year later, two years later, and now, new shopping centers continue to pop up within a few miles of my shop and the anticipation and excitement always seems to go where something new is happening. Not only do I hear people talk about it, I feel it too. There's a burrito place opening up very soon that I'm dying to check out.

Let's get back to that major misconception of retail, that "build-it-and-they-will-come" mentality. It is probably one of biggest myths in retail, and the one that gets the most people into trouble. They don't realize the amount of time and effort they will need to devote to marketing after they've built it. Marketing is a constant activity – whether you've just opened or are several years into your business.

What happens when you let up? At the start of our third Christmas season, I found myself in the hospital for a week and confined to the bed and couch for almost two weeks after and it took awhile to really get my strength and energy back.

The day-to-day business of the store went on just fine (thanks to the great employees I had!), but since I was the person responsible for marketing, that wasn't getting done. Specifically, email newsletters weren't going out, new flyers weren't made, and special activities that I wanted to plan for winter break didn't get planned.

The result: a very un-spectacular Christmas season in terms of gross sales.

Since then, I've tried to plan marketing activities further in advance, and give more marketing related tasks to my employees. For example, I'll come up with a flyer or mailing, and turn it over to them to have printed and mailed.

Yes, we have a website! Of *course* we have a website! **www.potandbead.com**

I don't care who you are, where you're located, what kind of business you're in: You Must Have A Website. Period. Don't let anyone convince you otherwise.

Also, don't let anyone convince you that you *must* spend a fortune to have one, or to have a decent one. Yes, to a large degree, you get what you pay for. But this is definitely one area where a start-up business can scrimp and do something very cheap at the beginning just to have something there.

When you're choosing a name for your business, consider choosing your website address at the same time. Ideally, you want them to be one and the same – it makes it easier for people to look you up and tell others about you.

Many, many, many good books have been written about how to set up a website, so I won't go into all the details of how to do it here.

I will tell you that once you have your website up, make sure it has the following:

- Your address and phone number prominently displayed! This is not information that someone should have to hunt for.
- If your business is one with regular hours (as opposed to, say, a consultant), again, make those super easy to find.
- Put your website address on everything else! Business cards, flyers, advertisements… anything that will get into the hands of potential customers.

Once your website is set up, there are ways to adver-tise it online like the "Cost-per-Click" advertising systems that Google and Yahoo offer. When you set up this kind of advertising account, you essentially say, "I want people who search for X to see my ad," where "X" is your product or service. So, your ad pops up when people search for "X" and you pay if and when the person actually clicks on your ad, taking them to your website.

Managing your online ads is actually a little more complicated and takes some effort on your part to set up the correct search words and ad text, but you get the idea.

Did you read Chapter 7 on Customers? Here's where keeping track of all that customer data becomes really important: Targeted Marketing.

We want to bring customers in with the least amount of money and effort, right? One of the best ways to do that is to focus on customers you already have, and try to let them know about new products or services that are similar to ones they've purchased from you before.

For example, all those customers who purchased a toothbrush holder in 2003 might be interested in the new soap dish we just got in.

Or all those customers who attended one of our special events might want to know that we're holding another special event.

When things like this happen, we might send out an invitation to just those customers instead of our whole database, or a random selection of people in the town. We target 100 customers who've purchased the product or service before, who we believe would purchase again instead of send out 10,000 mailings to people we don't know.

Remember, marketing is important to *any* and *every* business venture. Writing this book is another excellent example. My time and money went into this project, the book got published, and is for sale. So I need to tell people about it, I need to get the word out. (How did you find out about this book? Who put it in your hand?) If you're reading this, then however you found out about it, you did, therefore some form of marketing worked. That's wonderful!

I hope that you're enjoying it, and tell someone else about it. Or tell them about the website:

**www.cutelittlestore.net**

The Good:
- Marketing is where you can unleash your creative side.
- If you're doing it right, you can boost your sales – always a good thing!

The Bad:
- You can never stop marketing. You can never take a break. It's nearly impossible to sit back and relax.

Final Tidbits:

Marketing is an on-going effort for the small business owner. You can't rely on the "build-it-and-they-will-come" theory. They won't come if they don't know about you, think about you, remember you or have a good reason to.

# Chapter 10
## Hard Work Does Not Equal Money In Your Pocket

George I., who had recently sold his successful small medical practice and was on his way to a secure and active retirement asked me: "For love or money?"

I replied, chuckling a little, "For love OF money."

The reality is, if there wasn't at least the potential to make more money then we have right now, we wouldn't be in business for ourselves. It might not be on the very top of the priority list, but it's going to be in the top three, right? You can admit it. There's no shame in that. If money turns out to be your *only* motivation, then there might be a problem.

"It takes money to make money" is probably one of the most true statements I've ever heard.

The Pot & Bead was initially financed mostly with a Small Business Administration (SBA)-guaranteed loan. Many people get this confused with an "SBA loan." In general, the SBA isn't in the business of loaning out money themselves, although they do have some special programs like micro-loans.

What the SBA actually does is guarantee loans. What does this mean? This means that if my business goes under and I am unable to repay the loan, the SBA guarantees 85% of it to the bank. Meaning, the bank will be able to get 85% of their money back from the SBA. The catch that most people don't realize at the beginning is that you're still required to pay the SBA back.

There were various things we didn't know when we started the loan application process. The first, that took me a while to understand, was the issue of collateral. When you have an SBA-guaranteed loan, if you have collateral, you need to put it up to secure the loan. At the time, I was recently married and my husband and I had just bought a house. We had very little equity in it. This was also the time when interest rates were declining to (near) record lows. We were under the impression that you didn't need to put your house up as collateral for this kind of loan. We had that impression because we knew other people who did not own a house and had no significant collateral who had an SBA-guaranteed loan. We learned that the deal is that the SBA does not require a home or significant collateral, but if you have it, you need to put it up.

My now ex-husband, at the time, was not the most supportive person in this venture. We also mistakenly thought that since he wasn't 100% on board with my opening a store that he wouldn't need to be involved at all. I thought my business affairs were mine alone and he wouldn't need to sign things. Wrong again. The fact that we were married made the business a joint asset – he was just as legally and personally responsible as I was. This meant that he had to sign the loan and the lease. My business partner's spouse had to as well.

One mistake we made was in not really shopping around for a bank. One of the first things you'll read about in most books on starting a business is that you shouldn't necessarily go with the first bank that says yes. You can shop around for rates and terms.

Not so easy in practice when you're anxious to get your business started! We submitted applications to two banks at the same time, and were in the process of going around collecting the paperwork to submit more at other banks.

The first bank said no. Now chances are, you're going to get some "Nos." It happens all the time in life – college applications, job interviews, etc. It is, however, a bit of a blow to the ego.

Once this starts to happen, you get worried. Is *anyone* going to give us a loan? Will it happen on our timescale? We wanted to be in business by the start of the Christmas shopping season – would it happen? We couldn't sign a lease without a loan commitment.

So, when the second bank said "Yes!" (and their terms were reasonable) we abandoned all plans to pursue working with any other bank, meaning we didn't apply at any additional banks.

Obviously, because I'm telling you this, there were problems. The first problem was what most people go through when they are doing something new: we didn't know the right questions to ask. Therefore, we didn't get all the information we needed at the beginning. This really just affected our (specifically, my) stress level during the loan process.

The one big question I recommend asking is: What should we expect during this process? (Meaning: How long should it take?) Other related questions to ask are: Will I (and possibly my spouse) need to take time off work to sign papers? Are there papers we need to gather ahead of time to make the process go much faster?

Knowing what to expect would have taken away a lot of the stress and saved a couple of "Oh, I didn't know you needed that piece of paper," which dragged the process out much longer than was really necessary.

One of the questions we did ask was whether or not we'd be able to refinance our homes. After all, this was during a recent period of time when interest rates kept dropping. We were told by the bank that it wouldn't be a problem. When it's time to refinance, apparently the bank temporarily "lifts" the loan off the house for a day so the refinance can happen, then puts the loan back on.

Well, it was a problem. My husband and I were not able to refinance our home. Now that's stress. To this day, I'm still not 100% sure why it didn't happen. The mortgage company had all the papers and were ready to go to closing, but then no one (not me, my husband, or the mortgage company) could get a hold of anyone at the bank. No one at the bank would call us back.

A little more than a year later, I wound up re-financing the business loan with another bank. This time I shopped around – actually, I had met several bankers through the local Chamber of Commerce I belong to. One in particular, and his family, had been one of my first customers at the store. I felt that because of this, he knew and understood my business and business concerns a little better. So I wound up banking at his bank. (The terms and rates were slightly better too.) Relationships in business are very important. From day one, anyone looking to go into business for themselves should be cultivating helpful and productive relationships with others in their community.

One major thing we did *right* with the business loan was to get a loan that included enough working capital to get through the first several months. The very first thought we had when we knew we had to seek a loan was to only apply for the startup expenses. My accountant pointed out to us that this was not a good idea. Lots of businesses fail because they don't have enough working capital. Meaning they did not have enough money to pay expenses for some period of time while building up the business and building sales.

So we made sure that our loan included not only our startup expenses, but enough capital to cover us for approximately the first six months of business. I'm not sure we would have survived without that.

Another thing we did right was to have an accountant work with us from the beginning. He helped put together the financial section of the business plan, and has been with me ever since.

But, of course, there were a bunch of mistakes that were made with money after the store opened. Some of these involved personal finances – remember that I had recently given up my engineering job and salary so my personal finances and habits went through a drastic change. It took a while to get used to.

During the time period when I was still getting used to my new life, one mistake I made was buying a new car. I had paid off my old car a few months before the store opened. (Getting rid of debt is good!) For some reason, about two months after we opened, I was convinced that I had to buy a new one. It was a completely emotional decision.

I was tired, and working so much, I hadn't done a single fun thing for myself in months. Somehow, buying a new car made sense to me at the time. About six months later, it became clear that taking on additional unnecessary debt in the first year of starting up my business was a horrible mistake.

After three years, though I still acknowledge it was a mistake, it's one that has passed. If I could go back in time, I wouldn't have done it, but now I'm not feeling the pressure of the monthly payment anymore.

As a small business owner, money is always on your mind in some form or another. (Cute Little Tidbit: Purchasing good accounting software, like Quickbooks, is a must and absolutely should go in your startup budget.) Here are some items you need to be concerned with as a business or Cute Little Store owner. (There are several books out there that can help you lay out the way a startup budget and forecast for your business should look. (See Appendix A.) However, they don't give the prospective new business owner an idea of the numbers that go in there – that will take research on your part):

Paying yourself: I put this one first since it's probably the first question one who is contemplating a new business wants answered. How much can I pay myself? It's going to vary, business by business, but going into something new, you shouldn't expect to pay yourself for a year or more. Yep – I said a *year* or *more*. So start saving now… before you quit that day job, make sure you have enough in the bank to pay your own living expenses for that period of time. (This includes paying down personal debt like credit cards and car loans and not taking on new debt like I did.)

Paying employees: How much depends on a lot of things like experience level and local going rate. Make sure you're aware of your local, state, and the current federal minimum wage. Make sure you're aware of the regulations governing employees and things like how and when you can (or are in some cases required to) pay overtime. See The U.S. Department of Labor's website (http://www.dol.gov/esa/whd/) for a good introduction to things you need to know about paying employees. For my own business, payroll is my highest expense after rent.

Accountants: If you're not one yourself, then you're probably not an expert on taxes. If for no other reason, this is why you should hire an accountant. Mistakes can be costly! The best way to find a good accountant is to ask other local small business owners who they use. A good accountant can also help you understand the entire financial picture of your business. The going rate for an accountant varies by location. Ask around to get an idea of the rate.

Taxes: There's a colorful array of federal, state, and local taxes that businesses are subject to, which vary from state to state and county to county. For this reason, I highly recommend seeking out a good accountant to help. No matter where you're located, it's likely that there will be at least one type of tax that's due monthly (like sales tax) and there are several federal taxes due quarterly. My accountant visits me once a month to prepare all the tax returns. I just write the checks and get them in the mail. When I first opened the shop, I thought I would do it myself, but it was way too confusing. (Did I mention I'm an engineer with a degree in physics? I'm not stupid, but I couldn't figure this tax thing out.)

Your personal taxes also become more complicated now. Before owning The Pot and Bead, I did my personal tax returns on my own. Now, the accountant does them, too.

If you estimate how much your sales are per month, then you can estimate your sales tax. Other taxes can come out to be up to as much as a few thousand dollars, quarterly! (They depend on your sales, payroll, etc.)

Insurance: You need insurance. What kind and how much will depend on the kind of business you have, your location, your financing, your landlord, etc. At a minimum, expect to have a business policy that covers your business property, and if you're working anywhere outside your house, expect to have some kind of accident liability policy. If you have financing from a bank loan, you will likely be required to have a life insurance policy. If you have employees, you'll be required to provide Worker's Compensation insurance. The rules governing Worker's Compensation vary from state to state.

Your insurance agent should know the rules in your state. Don't be afraid to shop around for better rates or for an insurance agent you're comfortable working with.

Lawyers: Do you need to pay a lawyer? Sigh. There are a lot of books on starting your own small business that make it seem like you can do a lot of things on your own. There are books on "Legal Forms for Small Business" that are recommended as purchases and as a way to save money in the beginning.

I recommend that you read these books because they will give you some familiarity with some standard contracts like leases and sales agreements. But then when it comes down to it, you still want the lawyer to review any legal document that you might sign.

Just like when you're looking for an accountant, ask around to see who other small business owners use. When you're working with the lawyer, don't be afraid to ask ahead of time how much time they expect to spend reviewing something like your lease. If you think it's too long, say so. Find someone who you can really work with.

Credit Cards: You will likely need one for your business. Luckily, just like in your personal life, there are a lot of credit card offers out there that come with rewards like cash back on purchases or airline miles. But just as in your personal life, credit card debt is not good to carry around with you. Hopefully, before you start your business, you're free from any personal credit card debt.

Advertising Costs: We touched on this in the chapter on marketing. I'll repeat the important points here: 1) any marketing you can do for free should be done, 2) keep good records of what you paid and what business was generated from a particular advertisement, 3) keep records of other advertising offers (i.e., today you might not be interested in the package that was just sent to you about advertising on your local cable network, but tomorrow when you're planning, you might want to know how much it would have cost.)

Profit/Loss: ...or as it's usually called: P&L. This is one of several financial statements you'll want to review on a monthly basis to give you a financial picture of your business. Software like Quickbooks can output this report on request. There are several good books on small business finance that can help you learn to read this statement. (Some are listed in Appendix A.)

Budgeting: I found that this gets easier with time. The first year of business was an educated guess. After three years, I've got much more solid data to base my budget on. (i.e., I look at how much I spent on inventory in a certain month last year to have a gauge for how much I'll spend this year in that same month on inventory.)

Personal vs. Business Finance: These are unfortunately not always as separate as one might like them to be. I have my personal bank account, and I have a business bank account (with the business name and address and myself listed as the signatory). I have credit cards that once were personal, but are now used only for the business. Any credit extended to me for the business (this can be anything from a bank loan to setting up a utility, like the phone) goes on my personal credit report.

The good news is that many things that I used to pay for personally can be paid for by the business, like gas for the car and my cell phone. They're used for the business, so they're business expenses.

Borrowing From Relatives/Friends: There's good and bad here. Many books on financing the small business recommend seeking out relatives and friends that will help finance your business with a personal loan.

While there are many benefits, like the fact that this loan won't show up on your credit report and your family probably won't repossess your house if your business fails and you can't pay the loan back, there's an emotional side to consider too.

What happens to your relationship with this person if you can't pay the loan back right away or ever? Will it be forever damaged?

If you're going to borrow money from a family member or friend, there are two things you should do:

1) Get a loan agreement in writing. Agree on the amount and repayment terms and write it all down.
2) Make sure that this person can handle the risk. They are taking a risk. Make sure that if the worst happens – the business fails and the money is lost – that the person who lent it to you can live their life without it.

The Good:
- Accountants are helpful, especially if you're not an accountant or financial wizard yourself. An accountant is very useful in helping to sort out taxes, etc.
- It's true that you need to build relationships in business. (Especially with your banker.)

The Bad:
- Decisions based on emotion will bite back almost every time (i.e., settling for the first bank that says "Yes" to your loan application or making a major unnecessary purchase).
- Not having the capital to get you through the crucial startup phase of your business can kill your business in the first year!

Final Tidbits:

Keep your debt load as small as possible. Learn all you can about money and finances. Hire a good accountant and ask lots of questions.

# Chapter 11
## Other Things That Keep You Up At Night

We all handle stress in different ways. Stress affects me by keeping me from getting a good night's sleep. It's not always the big things that will do this to you, sometimes it's just the little things.

The point of this chapter is to make you aware of all the other little things that happen once you're the owner of that Cute Little Store. These are all the behind-the-scenes things that the customer who comes in and says, "You've got such a Cute Little Store here!" will never know about. These are the things that give you headaches and cause never-ending amounts of stress.

Water has been my arch-nemesis ever since my first apartment was flooded in college. Since then, no matter where I go, it seems determined to break my spirit.

At The Pot & Bead, within the first couple of months we had to have a plumber in to fix the toilet and back room sink. The sink still didn't work well for a long while after. The hot water refused to turn off all the way so we would use the off valve under the sink to control it. (I finally realized that instead of paying a plumber hundreds of dollars, I could buy a book on plumbing from Home Depot and fix it myself. That's just what I did.)

The hot water is also too hot. But on a busy Saturday during the winter months, we run out of hot water long before the day is over.

<u>Mini-Lessons Learned</u>: 1) In the lease, be clear of what the landlord will and will not be responsible for after you take possession of your space, 2) If you yourself are not handy with minor plumbing and electrical things, find a friend who is before running off to spend tons of money on a contractor. I've learned that many things that seem to be a big deal can be fixed on my own, or with the help of a friend.

Things will break when you least expect it. Make sure you or someone else is prepared to deal with that. This includes:
- Keep all the manuals in one place where anyone can access them.
- Empower employees to take action when something breaks.

<u>Mini-Lessons Learned</u>: Similar to above. Keep things written down. Know who can fix what. Teach employees to fix things.

Our computer, which we use as our cash register, needs rebooting a lot. Our kilns, which are our main production equipment, have broken. It seems like every other week it's something. Recently, one of my employees told me that the heat didn't seem to be working in the middle of winter. "Oh poo," I thought. (Okay, I'll admit... I said a word to myself that was much less polite than "poo.") Since our first winter, we knew that there was a flaw in the heating unit's circuit board, which required that occasionally we go into the circuit breaker box and flip a switch. At least a month earlier, I had told this employee about that over the phone. Now, with the heat not working again, she told me she had flipped the switch.

I figured that before I go call an expensive contractor (Cute Little Tidbit: I'm not implying that all contractors are really expensive, but when you planned on spending zero dollars, spending anything can sometimes be too much to handle emotionally and break the budget), I would try it for myself. I flipped the switch and viola! We had heat! (Turns out my employee hadn't flipped the right switch – apparently I wasn't that clear when I tried to explain over the phone.)

I was stressed out for an entire day for what thankfully turned out to be nothing.

<u>Mini-Lessons Learned</u>: Troubleshooting skills are important. Have backup plans available; have backup equipment, if possible. Stay calm and remember to laugh after the fact.

My cell phone. It's always on. I wish I could turn it off. But I can't. It's my business, it's my store, and at any point in time, something really bad can happen and I need to be reached.

Even when the store is closed, I can't turn it off. What if there's another burglary? They need to be able to reach me.

What if I'm going somewhere and I don't know if my cell phone will work? I have to prepare a backup plan. A different way for them to reach me if needed.

This is a constant source of stress that won't go away as long as I'm the business owner. It's something that I've gotten used to, I think. It doesn't keep me up at night anymore, but I do almost cringe every time my phone rings with the feeling of "What Now?" To get rid of that feeling, I always remind my employees that they're allowed to call me when something really good happens (like a customer just spent a lot of money, or they got wonderful compliments about the store, etc.), and they do.

Mini-Lessons Learned: Your business is part of your life and if certain aspects are a constant source of stress, you need to find a way to deal with that, or else it will burn you out. Find ways to turn negatives into positives.

There is an excellent book out there called *The Small Business Owner's Guide to Getting a Good Night's Sleep.* The point of that book is that lots of bad things can happen, yet you can be prepared for a lot of them.

It took me a long time to get through reading that book. Planning for the worst is an emotionally challenging thing to do. I could barely get through a chapter without becoming incredibly tense and stressed out. Finally, I convinced myself that several of the issues the book raised were ones I needed to deal with. Most are not too difficult, they just require some thought, and writing those thoughts down.

A lot of that deals with having procedures for worst case scenarios (if you don't even have procedures for basic day-to-day stuff, go back to Chapter 5 on Employees and read about why you need them).

The Good:
- All the little things that can happen and keep you up at night can be dealt with.

The Bad:
- All the little things that can happen DO happen, often when you least expect it (or five minutes after you thought you could go home for the day).

Final Tidbits:

The better prepared you are, the better you will sleep at night. You can practice laughing at my mishaps, in the hope that when it happens to you, you'll be able to laugh afterwards too.

# Chapter 12
## How To Survive Those First Two Years

After all the bad stuff that can happen, is it even *possible* to survive? Yes, absolutely. Read on for how to get a good start on your new business. Already in business? That's okay, you can still catch up and regain your sanity.

<u>Business Planning</u>
...is exactly what it sounds like: planning and research. This involves actually creating a business plan. I don't care what business you're in, you need a business plan. Let me say it again: YOU NEED A BUSINESS PLAN. That should always be the first step in starting your business. Find a small business that failed in the first two years and I'm almost willing to put money on there not having been a business plan.

If you go to a bank or other institution for a loan, they'll ask you to include a business plan with your loan application.

If you rent retail space, lots of landlords will ask to see your business plan as part of their decision making process.

If you don't need either of the above, you still need a business plan, but it probably doesn't have to be as elaborate. In this case, you are the reader and you can get away with a minimalist business plan. In this case, you need it for YOU. Your business plan will clearly define your business. It will outline your goals. Yes, you might have all that in your head. That's not good enough. Get it on paper. The act of putting things on paper solidifies your business concept, and can help you identify flaws before they sink your dreams.

If you don't have a business plan, go grab a couple sheets of paper. Yes, right now. Get a pen(cil), too.

On the top of the piece of the paper write the name of your new business. If you don't have a name, write something like "Adeena's Bookstore" (substitute "Adeena" with your name and "Bookstore" with whatever business you're planning).

Underneath, write one or two sentences about what the business actually is about.

"Adeena's Bookstore is/will be a specialty retail bookstore focusing on the science fiction and fantasy genres."

A friend of mine, who's now on his third business, learned the hard way the first time around. He had a great idea for a consulting/seminar business, and was so eager to get going that he just got going. He had no business plan, no financial plan, no plan to bring money in, but he was paying a lot of money out in advertising and other costs. He couldn't keep it up for too long before he realized it wasn't working out the way it was going. Luckily, he didn't lose too much money. But, he learned that he needed a business plan before starting his next business. (Also, luckily, this experience didn't kill his entrepreneurial spirit.)

If you need further help writing and developing your business plan, see Appendix A for a good reference. Your local small business development center is also a great resource.

Organization

I truly believe that at least 70% of running an operating business is keeping up with all the paperwork. Mail, bills, vendor catalogs, solicitations, applications, tax forms, advertising rate sheets, etc. build up VERY quickly.

Early on, ideally on day one, you'll want to establish a system for keeping yourself organized. Many papers in business can't be thrown away. A lot of papers you just won't want to throw away – what if that customer comes back? What if you want to compare this guy's advertising rates with someone else's? What did you buy last summer?

I started out with a small hanging file folder box which I quickly outgrew. I am now using heavy duty plastic stackable cabinets with hanging file folders. I like these better than the old-fashioned metal file cabinets because they're not as difficult to move around (as I found out recently when I rearranged my office at home).

This is one major area where WWFMMNWFY (What works for me may not work for you). But at the end of the day, you need to be organized.

What worked for me was actually hiring a professional organizer. This is someone that I routinely ran into at my local Chamber's networking events. After being in business less than a year, I had so many things to do that I was nearly paralyzed and felt like I couldn't get anything done. So I hired her to help me with organization and time management.

That was one of the best things I did for myself during that first year. (Cute Little Tidbit: A retail consultant I've worked with has a hard time believing that most small business owners don't devote any time or resources to continuing personal development.) She helped me consolidate and reorganize my to-do list and helped me realize that there isn't enough time to get EVERYTHING done, therefore everything can't be a #1 priority.

The next spring, through my local Chamber of Commerce, she was offering a three-part course on organization. The course covered some of the time management topics we worked on the previous summer as well as other physical organization skills. It was offered at a significant discount through the Chamber, so I went. (Cute Little Tidbit: A good Chamber is a good resource for the small business owner.) I'm glad I did. I was able to finally get my home office together. The previous month, my office had been such a disaster that it was preventing me from getting anything useful done. I couldn't even look in that room without feeling the stress piling up. It's much better now.

I liken organization to something like Weight Watchers. You don't go once and get fixed automatically. It's a constant process that involves some commitment and self-discipline, and you occasionally need outside reminders.

<u>Your Team of Experts</u>

Having a good accountant and a good lawyer are definitely the first places to start.

You can't be an expert on everything. There are areas of your business where you will need help. Developing good relationships with some key experts will definitely help to preserve some of your sanity and avoid mistakes.

During the early business planning stages, we read an article in a local newspaper about an accountant who recently went out on his own and specialized in helping small business startups. It was perfect. He was intimately involved in the earliest financial models for my business and is still my accountant today.

Finding a good lawyer was harder. That's mostly because of my own inner biases against lawyers – I always had this feeling that too many of them don't understand that I'm not wealthy and I don't have an unlimited amount of money to spend

So, initially, we didn't want a lawyer to do anything but the absolute minimum – help us set up an operating agreement and file the proper paperwork to form the Limited Liability Company (LLC).

However, as business developed and new things happened (see the chapter following your gut), I've come to realize that lawyers do perform a valuable service in today's society and economy.

Later, I realized that I wanted a lawyer who understood a little more about my business, who would be a little more involved, and who would be there as the business grew. I think I have that person now.

## Building a Support System

Your support system is made up of the people and things that will keep you sane. They might be your spouse, family or best friend. They might be the hobbies and things you like to do.

Make sure there's at least one person in your life that you can openly talk to about your business. Many times this would be your spouse. This should be someone not super involved in your business, but someone who's supportive nonetheless.

I have my significant other, my ex-husband, my father, and the rest of my family and friends. (I'm very lucky.)

It is lonely at the top, even if it's the top of a small business. I didn't think I was going to miss not having colleagues any more – not having those people to discuss my work with. I also didn't think I was going to miss one positive aspect of working for someone else: my own performance reviews. With a couple of the individuals I worked for, I found performance reviews very helpful. For me, they did provide some useful feedback and it was always good to hear that I was doing well.

There's no one around me now who tells me I'm doing a good job. The only way I ever know is if sales are good. Occasionally my ex-husband or dad says something nice, but it is rare. Overhearing customers saying nice things is usually good.

I think the best ones were this past summer when one of my wonderful, regular customers said to me: "This is my daughter's favorite place to come to."

## Putting Your Personal Finances In Order

It's funny. I'm telling you this and it's still something I have yet to master. It's one of those "if I could do it all again" things.

If I could do it all again, I would have done my best to get rid of all my credit card debt. I also would not have bought a new car that I really didn't need during the first couple of months of business operation.

Getting your finances in order will definitely have a humongous impact on surviving those early years.

Something that we did do right: my ex-husband and I bought a cheap home. I don't mean "cheap" as in quality. I mean we bought a house that cost less than half of what we were approved for. This was all before the business started and the business wasn't our motivation for doing that. But I'm glad we did... if we hadn't, I wouldn't have been able to quit my decently-salaried engineering job to make next-to-nothing.

One thing to realize is that reducing your income will take some getting used to, but you can do it.

You might even opt to sell your home for a less expensive one.

Just make sure you realize that in starting a business, you're taking a risk. Assume the worst, and understand what would happen if you're forced to close and liquidate your business.. What would this mean to your personal life? Are you able to keep the roof over your head?

## Keeping Yourself Healthy

Eat well. Exercise. Sleep. Everywhere you turn, you hear these things. Well, it's even more crucial when you're in business for yourself. If you're sick, who's taking care of your business?

The first winter we were open, I was pretty paranoid about getting sick. I took very large vitamin C pills several times a day. I was really worried because for the first time in my adult life, I was being exposed to TONS of kids who all carry everything.

I did get a bit of sniffles that winter, but nothing terribly bad.

My 2nd year in business, I got a little lax in this area and wound up getting some bad colds that rendered me useless for several days.

<u>Stress-Relieving and Sanity-Keeping Techniques</u>

As I said in earlier in this chapter, WWFMMNWFY. What is true is that in starting your own small business, you'll have a lot of stress and you'll need to deal with it or seriously risk your health and/or business.

Some ideas and some things that work for me:
- Remind yourself why you're doing this. Think of the alternatives.
- Find an excuse to pamper yourself. Maybe a visit to a local day spa for a massage after your busy season.
- Drink tea. Green and other herbal teas are supposed to be healthy.
- Go to the gym. Exercise is a proven stress reliever.
- Remember what makes you smile or laugh.
- Take some time for yourself. You business is your priority and a major responsibility, but you can't obsess over it 24 hours a day, 365 days a year. Allow yourself some time to be "off."

The Good:
- You can give your new business venture the best chance of survival by planning well upfront.

The Bad:
- Lack of upfront planning can mean your business col-

lapses before it really ever had a chance.

A Final Tidbit:

Starting a business takes a lot of upfront planning to ensure that you'll survive the first couple of risky years. The more you are able to do ahead of time, the better off you'll be.

# Chapter 13
## So You Still Want Your Own Cute Little Store

So you've read this entire book of good and bad, and you still want your own Cute Little Store or other small business. You've decided that you can handle the bad in order to get the good. Kudos! You're on your way.

Before you rush off, answer the following questions for yourself (Cute Little Tidbit: not all of them have right or wrong answers):

Why do you want your own Cute Little Store? List the reasons.

_____

_____

_____

_____

What is your current financial situation?

_____

_____

_____

_____

_____

In order to support yourself and possibly your family, do you need to continue to take in whatever income you take in now? (If the answer to this question is yes, but you still want to go into business for yourself, start working NOW on reducing your debt and building up a savings cushion that can carry you through the first year of your business.)

_____

_____

_____

_____

_____

Do you have any debt? If so, start reducing that NOW. Debt can be a serious block to getting any financing necessary for your business.

_____

_____

_____

_____

_____

Do you have a spouse or significant other who would be involved (even indirectly)? Have you spoken with him or her about your idea and desire?

_____

_____

_____

_____

_____

Are you in good physical shape? (Do you eat right and exercise?) If the answer is no, consider working on this. Even if your business will not have you on your feet the whole day, the better physical condition you are in, the better you will be able to handle any stress that comes your way!

_____

_____

_____

_____

_____

How organized are you?

_____

_____

_____

_____

List of Things to Have Before opening or purchasing a business:
- a business plan!
- zero (or as close as possible) debt
- supportive family and friends

Remember that there is List of On-Going Responsibilities that you as the owner will constantly have to deal with:
- employee management
- customer service/appreciation
- marketing
- paying the bills
- finding new ways to boost sales
- keeping track of financials, inventory, customers, etc.

# Appendix A
## The Reading List

*Pour Your Heart Into It: How STARBUCKS Built a Company One Cup at a Time* by Howard Schultz and Dori Jones Yang. Hyperion: 1997.

Adeena's Tidbit: A very inspiring book. If a guy from the Brooklyn projects can become this successful, so can anyone.

*The E-Myth Revisited: Why Most Small Businesses Don't Work and What to Do About It* by Michael E. Gerber. Collins: 1995.

Adeena's Tidbit: This is an absolute must read. I'm amazed how many people who think about or start their own business who don't know about this book. Michael Gerber describes in detail the differences between working "on" versus "in" a business and I like to think my business is an example of one that has taken Mr. Gerber's advice to heart and is doing it right.

*Don't Worry, Make Money: Spiritual and Practical Ways to Create Abundance and More Fun in Your Life* by Richard Carlson. Hyperion: 1997.

Adeena's Tidbit: If you're obsessed with making money, if all you can think about is what you're not making and why you're not making more, this book is for you.

*The Small Business Owner's Guide to a Good Night's Sleep: Preventing and Solving Chronic and Costly Problems* by Debra Koontz Traverso. Bloomberg Press: 2001.

Adeena's Tidbit: I've referred to this book quite a bit. Suffice to say, it's a must-have on the small business owner's bookshelf.

*The Retail Life: A Store Manager's Companion* by Tierney Alexander. Writer's Club Press: 2002.

Adeena's Tidbit: The small business owner often acts as the manager too, particularly in a Cute Little Store. I swear I could have written some of the chapters in this book – especially the one on employees.

*The Profitable Retailer: 56 surprisingly simple and effective lesions to boost your sales and profits* by Doug Fleener. Acanthus Publishing: 2005.

Adeena's Tidbit: Doug Fleener is a retail consultant who I've hired to help me with my business at times. Anything Doug writes or says is worth reading and listening to.

*How To Buy a Business* by Richard A. Joseph, Anna M. Nekoranec and Carl H. Steffens. Kaplan Publishing: 1992.

Adeena's Tidbit: There's a whole chapter on the concept of "due diligence."

*Retail Business Kit for Dummies* by Rick Segel. For Dummies: 2001.

Adeena's Tidbit: If you are truly starting from scratch when it comes to understanding the financials of a business, start here. This book also contains a "S.W.O.T." exercise.

*Legal Guide for Starting & Running a Small Business* by Fred S. Steingold and Ilona M. Bray. NOLO: 2005, 8th edition.

Adeena's Tidbit: I consider this book a must have for any small business owner. It doesn't replace using a lawyer, but gives a good explanation so you know when to spend your money on one. This book also has a good chapter on understanding commercial leases.

*Business Plans for Dummies* by Paul Tiffany and Steven D. Peterson. For Dummies: 2004, 2nd edition.

Adeena's Tidbit: If you haven't thought about writing a business plan before, start here.

*Start Run & Grow a Successful Small Business* by CCH Incorporated. CCH Incorporated: 2005, 5th edition.

Adeena's Tidbit: While not focused solely on retail business, this book has an excellent chapter on business plans and more detail on understanding the financials of a business than *Retail Business Kit for Dummies*.

*The Small Business Bible: Everything You Need To Know To Succeed In Your Small Business* by Steven D. Strauss. John Wiley & Sons: 2004.

Adeena's Tidbit: This book has a good chapter on "your web presence."

# Index

CPSIA information can be obtained at www.ICGtesting.com
Printed in the USA
BVOW071610151211

278445BV00001B/95/A